AF560371

GLOBAL VIOLENCE, PEACE AND SECURITY

GLOBAL VIOLENCE, PEACE AND SECURITY

Editor

RANJAN GARG

Head, Department of Political Science
Malwa College, Bondli, Samrala (Punjab)

REGAL PUBLICATIONS

New Delhi

GLOBAL VIOLENCE, PEACE AND SECURITY

ISBN 978-81-8484-519-8

Typeset by
RAHUL COMPOSERS
New Highway Apartments, Lakshmi Niwas
760, Pocket-D, Lok Nayak Puram, New Delhi - 110 041

Printed in India at
MAYUR ENTERPRISES
WZ Plot No. 3, Gujjar Market, Tihar Village, New Delhi - 110 018

Published by
REGAL PUBLICATIONS
F-159, Rajouri Garden, New Delhi - 110 027
Phone : 45546396, 25435369
E-mail : regalbookspub@yahoo.com, regaldeepbooks@yahoo.com

Dedicated To

The next generation of my family.....

Amulya, Riya, Shreya, Vanshika,
Tanishtha, Saksham and Manan

Contents

Preface

The twentieth century is a century of progress in the fields of political, scientific, technological, social and economic spheres. It has also witnessed the concretisation of great ideas like globalisation and liberalisation. It has brought the countries together and turning the whole world into a global village. These tremendous changes gave birth to new culture, i.e. the culture of materialism and consumerism. However, these changes have failed to bring equity, peace and harmony in the society rather it has resulted in serious social, political and economic imbalances, problems and value crises. The man has acquired material wealth and conforts but the whole world appears to be divided into racial, religions, castes, classes and ethnic groups. The world is passing through all round unrest such as terrorism, nuclear war and regional wars, etc. Sometimes it seems that brutality has dominated over the humanity, barbarian activities, malice sense, etc. have been inherited in the psyche of selfish persons that has created problems.

It is paradoxical that on one hand the human being has grown as the most developed and intelligent species ever existed on the earth but on the other hand he has become extremely self-centred, individualistic, intolerant and even self-destructive. While men have created many technological inventions they can not be able to 'create' peace. Scientists have unleashed the power of atom but are powerless to unleash peace upon earth. The biggest danger in front of us today is that Violence and Science both joined hands together not only to destroy the peace of universe but also to threaten the very existence of humanity. Due to this we have lost our security and peace. It has become increasingly important that we find ways to live together with peace in a secure world. We want to create a 'True World' where every individual is at peace hence feel secure.

A desperate need, therefore is being felt by educationists, philosophers, scientists and political leaders to rejuvenate the human values, which may bring long-lasting peace on this planet.

The concept of peace, by and large has remained an elusive concept which has many interpretations ranging from as simple as absence of conflict or war to as complex as the ability to cope with it. Peace has also been associated with inner peace throughout the ages. Many religions of the world propounded this concept of peace. Peace is often regarded as 'Absentia Belli', means the absence of any organised violence. Another version of peace forwarded by John Galtung, noted peace research scholar, peace is when there is no violence in the structure of society itself. It is present when human beings are being influenced so that their actual somatic and mental realizations are below their potential realizations. Some scholars view 'Peace as Justice' others look at it from the point of view to be secure in the war like situation.

How to achieve peace in this troublesome world has been the age old problem. The individual spiritual transformation and the transformation of modern violent social structures are inseparable. So the two dimensions of peace should be seen as two sides of the same coin.

Peace is important for humankind because we need a better world for our next generation. It is a basic requirement for our existence. Peace by its nature brings lot of joys. It is not a concept, it is an idea, it is not a luxury, it is a necessity. Everybody needs a peaceful life for themselves, their families, community and society. Yet every persons idea of peace varies according to their nation, culture and upbringing.

The challenges of our time have become so multifarious, multidimensional and mind boggling that no clear direction seems to be emerging. What is more they give us contradictory and conflicting horizons. Mankind finds itself under severe stress and pain and compelled to reassess International Scenario and its various conflicting values. In such a situation, the only hope left is philosophy of M.K. Gandhi. His concept of Truth and Non-violence give solace to all those who seek happiness, real prosperity and goodwill for all.

Dr. J.N. Sharma, Professor, Gandhian Studies Department, Panjab University, Chandigarh emphasized in his paper that in the age of conflicts within each nation, problem can't be solved through military dictatorship or war. Tolstoy and Gandhi regarded war as "human killing human", is a social disease. He discussed two versions on the subject of war and conflicts. First, conflict is endemic to human society as long as there are people in the world there will be conflicts. The another version is, the final goal of society is to be minimally without warfare and maximally without conflicts. Non-violence is always better than war. Though men and women preached peace yet they could never desist from waging war against mankind.

Dr. Hardarshan Kaur, Principal of Bhutta College of Education, Ludhiana, stressed on the need of education for peace. Peace education is the process of promoting knowledge, skills, attitudes and values needed to bring about behavioural changes that will enable children, youth and adults to prevent conflicts and to resolve conflicts peacefully. By developing attitudes of mutual respect and cooperation among students we can make them socially mature rather than growing them as egoistic and self-centred individuals.

Gandhi was never a crusader for peace so much as a non-violent warrior in the cause of justice, stressed Dr. Kiran Chauhan, department of Gandhian Studies, Panjab University, Chandigarh. Gandhi declared himself to be against the 'peace of grave' Satyagraha and Non-violence turns out to be fundamental techniques or methods adopted in pursuit of social reconstruction and justice. He was not so much a fighter for peace as a peaceful fighter for justice. He felt that perfect peace was an unattainable perfect Ideal.

Dr. Suresh Soni, Associate Professor, Govt. College, Jhandutta, Distt. Bilaspur (H.P) in his article is of the view that modern sophisticated weapons are a threat to the entire mankind. By peace, we don't mean absence of overt violence only but also eradication of roots of violence, such as social and economic exploitation, injustice and inequality. Choice before the mankind is between Non-violence or Non-existence. The best society provides to its citizens peace, opportunities and development of personality. The construction of bombs and weapons are indicators of wiping out entire mankind. To save ourselves from this mankind should adopt policies of M.K. Gandhi.

Dr. Sanjeev Kumar Sharma, Assistant Professor, Department of History, Govt. College, Ambala Cantt (Haryana) points out that the 20th century was bloodiest and most destructive century in the history of human race. There is no winner or loser in nuclear war. Both the nations at war would be annihilated. Gandhian concept of non-violence is the only hope left to save the mankind from violence and extinction. Peace is the catch word in International relations because the world has come to realize more than ever the vital role of peace in the survival of mankind.

In his article, Dr. Ramesh Kumar, Assistant Professor, Department of History, Govt. College, Chachrauli (Haryana) discussed to what extent Gandhi's idea on the settlement of conflicts has been accepted. He stressed on the need that workers in industry must be given a sense of belongingness to the factory in which they work. The political leadership must be able to convince public opinion that the elimination of strikes is in the interest of all. Gandhi's theory of trusteeship is still relevant in the 21st century, for the successful implementation of law. Some conditions are essential like unreasonable delays to be avoided, confidence in third party judgment, panel of arbitrators should be kept upto date and settlement of disputes amicably, etc.

Dr. Monica Sharma, Director, Centre for Gandhian Studies, Kanya Mahavidhyalya, Jalandhar (Punjab) is of the opinion that in modern society full of crises, scams, violence and destruction, can we achieve peace and harmony in this scenario? Peace education is the only solution left behind. Gandhian ideas of peace can be of great help in cultivating the culture of peace in next generation.

Ms. Shivali Kapoor, research scholar at University of Jammu, Jammu (J&K) discussed the idea of security without violence, i.e. human security. She discussed the traditional concept of security that is limited to the protection of states and its boundaries by preparing armed forces. The changing concept of security laid more stress on the security of humans rather than security of borders. Gandhiji is also in favour of human security. He said weapons can't provide security to the individuals. Weapons provide more insecurity among states. For the peaceful world order, Gandhi wants it should be non-violent, non-exploitative and cooperative based on reforms through education.

Mr. Suresh Kumar Jaglan, Research Scholar, Department of Gandhian Studies, Panjab University, Chandigarh discussed peace and human security in a different perspective. Traditionally peace is understood in military terms now-a-days, peace means existence of a political and economic environment where each individual is truly free from the control of any powerful person or a powerful nation. Both the trends of violence and of peace have gone together in human history. If there is violence in society then there are sages, prophets, thinkers, writers, poets and saints too who emphasized love, peace and harmony.

Dr. Mouha Khosla, Assistant Professor in Malwa Central College of Education for Women, Ludhiana (Punjab), stressed on the need of promoting peace through education. Peace education is teaching the information, attitude, values and behavioural competencies needed to resolve conflicts without violence and to built and maintain mutual beneficial harmonious relationships. It can provide answer to all problems—from injustice to poverty, from personal anxiety to inter personal conflicts, from neighbourhood misunderstanding to international tensions.

Another Research Scholar from Gandhian Studies Department, Panjab University, Chandigarh stressed on the relevance of Non-violence in Modern Times. If today the world has a number of problems that seems to be very complicated and insoluble, it is because, we are in the age of disbelief, mistrust and violent attitudes towards those problems. What we require today is the harmonious blending or creative synthesis of the results of modern science and technology and spiritual values. Gandhian technique of Non-violence can be the tool to attain peace in the society.

Ms. Anita Rathore, Assistant Professor in Sociology at Govt. Degree College, Theog, Distt. Shimla (H.P.) is of the view that remarkable development of science and technology during the last two centuries has further contributed to the misery caused by war. The road towards happiness and peace can come through the philosophy of Humanism rather than any religion.

Dr. Preeti Singh, Department of Political Science, Vasanta College for Women, Rajghat, Varanasi (U.P) argues that role of women in building a peaceful society. Despite significant relations between gender and peace, gender issues remained excluded from dominant peace discourses for a long time. Peace studies has much to gain by including women's voice. Need is to add women's perspective in peace studies and to move ahead from mere adding women to peace studies.

Ms. Sangeeta, Assistant Professor at Malwa College, Bondli-Samrala, District Ludhiana (Punjab) points out that peace is the need of an hour. Only slogans for 'Peace' can't change the society. We need to work for it by cultivating humanistic education by covering various aspects responsible for creating social discontents. The life and teachings of Gandhi can be a beacon of hope and courage to all of us.

Mr. Vijay Chauhan, Assistant Professor, Department of Political Science, Dyal Singh College, Karnal (Haryana) discussed India's regional security issues. In the first part of his article, he discussed national security and in the later half he examined the India's regional concerns in the long-run and in broader perspective, he laid stress on the issues like secessionist movements and insurgences in the world, bilateral issues with Pakistan, China, Sri Lanka, Bangladesh, Nepal and Afghanistan. India needs to tackle these issues responsibly as it will be in its own national interest to have peaceful neighbours.

Dr. Ghanshyam Dev, Associate Professor, Department of Political Science, DAV College, Sector 10, Chandigarh discussed Gandhian vision of human security. While elaborating the various issues concerning National Security, he concluded that state centric view of security has a very little concern about human beings and human security. Gandhian human security considers state as means rather than an end. 'End' is good life free from all insecurities and violence.

Ms. Anu Sharma, Assistant Professor, Rayat Bahra College of Education, Mohali (Punjab) laid stress on the concept of human security as a goal to attain peaceful society. The concept of security is not new to social sciences. Traditional security paradigm focuses on security of states instead of security of humans. She also discussed the concept of human security in the period of cold war and post-cold war era.

I wish to acknowledge my gratitude to Professor Dr. J.N. Sharma, Department of Gandhian Studies, Panjab University, Chandigarh for his guidance, sustained encouragement, constructive criticism and trust in my abilities at every stage of my work. He himself is an epitome of peace and a beacon light for many national and international research scholars.

I am also thankful to my family especially my mother Mrs. Chanchal Aggarwal and my son Amulya for their kind cooperation, sincerity and affection at every step of my life.

I am also grateful to my friends especially Mouha, Ghansham, Gurinder, Jagmohan Singh, Jaspal Singh, Amir Singh and V.K. Mehta for always being very affectionating and caring to me.

I am very thankful to the management of Malwa College, Bondli-Samrala especially Sardar Balbir Singh Rajewal and his team in the college for their overwhelming support and encouragement during my work.

Lastly, I am also thankful to Regal Publications, New Delhi for their consistence zeal in printing and publication of this book.

RANJAN GARG

List of Contributors

Ms. **Anita Rathore**, Assistant Professor (Sociology), Government Degree College, Theog, Distt. Shimla (H.P.).

Mrs. **Anu Sharma**, Assistant Professor, Rayat Bahra College of Education, Sahauran, Distt. Mohali (Punjab).

Dr. **Ghanshyam Dev**, Head, Department of Political Science, DAV College, Chandigarh.

Dr. **Hardarshan Kaur**, Principal, Bhutta College of Education, Ludhiana (Punjab).

Dr. **Jai Narain Sharma**, Professor, Department of Gandhian & Peace Studies, Panjab University, Chandigarh.

Dr. **Kiran Chauhan**, Department of Gandhian & Peace Studies, Panjab University, Chandigarh.

Dr. **Mohua Khosla**, Assisstant Professor, Malwa Central College of Education for Women, Ludhiana (Punjab).

Dr. **Monica Sharma**, Director, Gandhian Studies Centre, KMV, Jalandhar (Punjab).

Dr. **Preeti Singh**, Department of Political Science, Vasanta College for Women, Rajghat, Varanasi (U.P.).

Dr. **Ramesh Kumar**, Assist. Professor, Departmemt of History, Government College, Chachrauli (Haryana).

Dr. **Ranjan Garg**, HOD, Political Science, Malwa College, Bondli-Samrala Distt., Ludhiana (Punjab).

Ms. **Sangeeta**, Assistant Professor (History), Malwa College, Bondli-Samrala Distt., Ludhiana (Punjab).

Dr. **Sanjeev Kumar Sharma**, Assistant Professor, Department of History, Government College, Ambala Cantt (Haryana).

Ms. Shivali Kapoor, Research Scholar, Department of Political Science, University of Jammu, Jammu (J & K).

Mr. Suresh Kumar Jaglan, Research Scholar, Department of Gandhian and Peace Studies, Panjab University, Chandigarh.

Dr. Suresh Soni, Associate Professor, Government College, Jhandutta, Distt. Bilaspur (H.P.).

Dr. Vijay Chauhan, Assistant Professor, Department of Political Science, Dyal Singh College, Karnal (Haryana).

Mr. Waseem Saeed, Research Scholar, Department of Gandhian and Peace Studies, Panjab University, Chandgarh.

Human Survival and Peace Keeping 1

JAI NARAIN SHARMA

We are living today in an age of conflicts-conflicts within each nations: there are the problems of castes and economic classes, of the haves and have-nots, which some people feel can be solved only through civil strife. Then there are the problems of the rights of religious and racial minorities in some countries, as in South Africa, it is not minority but majority rights that are at stake. Further, there is the question whether democracy is not a tardy and slow-moving machine? and whether things cannot be ordered more quickly and efficiently under military dictatorship or under a dictatorship of the right or the left? It is becoming more and more difficult for people concerned with their immediate needs and handicaps in life to realize that in the long-run democracy is a more stable, progressive and educative form of government than autocracy or dictatorship. In the international field there are the problems of imperialism and colonialism of the old and the new communist varieties and of countries forcibly divided and kept divided, of armaments of a nature which if used will destroy all the progress that humanity has made through the centuries and even destroy mankind overnight. For these and many other national and international problems which keep coming up there seems to be no solutions in sight. As a matter of fact, today there are only problems and no solutions! The old, ultimate solution through violence and war is neither desirable nor practical. War today is a spent-out historical device for establishing right and justice. Whatever constructive value it had in the past of righting wrongs and establishing justice and equality, today it is only a destructive force. It solves no problems. Rather it creates more problems than it solves. It has committed, as it were, suicide, 'through the very monstrosity of the weapons that have made available by Science and Technology.

However, it is not possible for men and women to live under conditions of cruelity, injustice and tyranny for long, without devising means to remove them. To allow these to remain un-remedied, because they cannot be solved without violence and war, will be an advice of despair which, however, temporarily acquiesced in, can never be a permanent solution. Throughout the centuries the best spirit of the age have worked for freedom, justice and equality. It is impossible that humanity, without abrogating its claim to be human, can give up the struggle or the effort to create a more just and a more worthy world to live in. As a matter of fact, the moral and spiritual justification for the existence of human beings on earth would disappear if they did not work for noble ends. If then the old methods of hate, violence and war serve higher purposes no more, is it not incumbent upon the intelligent, thoughtful and morally sensitive people everywhere to find some new methods which will solve our problems and cure our ills without killing the patient in the process? I should like to suggest that there is such a new method which humanity can try without annihilating itself through unclear weapons—the method of diminishing national and international tensions and avoiding strife and violence, which was tried in India with some success under the leadership of Gandhi, whom we in affection and reverence call the Father of our nation.[1]

All right-thinking people are agreed that full-scale warfare would spell the extinction of the human race, at least in the form in which we have known it so far. Since the end of the Second World War which concluded with the inauguration of the nuclear age, the definition of war, as a 'continuation of policy by other means' contains within it a literally self-annihilating contradiction: a nuclear war would not merely be the end rather than the continuation of policy, but the end of the disputing parties as well.

Not only are the consequences of nuclear war too terrible to contemplate, the two world wars which we have already witnessed involved and affected combatant and civilian populations on an unprecedented scale, involving large numbers in scenarios of dehumanization and brutalization. Again there has been a bloody repetition in South-East Asia and the Middle East. Hiroshima opened bizarre horizons for humanity, but by no means is it possible to describe the preceding world wars or the Asian wars as 'civilized' though there may be worse degrees of barbarity yet to come.

Although it is unfortunately true that the ruthless and arrogant strategist or ideologue still regards 'limited' wars as 'acceptable' (acceptable to whom?), today advances in Military Science and technology bring large-scale suffering to whichever parties are involved in war. The sufferings and losses of the Vietnamese and Cambodians for instance have been more 'total' than 'limited'. Moreover, the interests of the superpowers being global, the possibility of escaiation of any so-called 'limited' conflict cannot be ruled out, so that the problem of this century is that of getting out of the 'war trap' not only war between the superpowers, but war between any powers. Today we are faced with the problem of bare human survival.

However, the above point of view, which looks upon war in any form, conventional or nuclear, 'limited' or global, as an unmitigated disaster, is not held by all people, whether decision-makers or otherwise. The meaning of war and its utility or disutility marks the subject of research not merely or an army of peace-makers, but regrettably also of war-makers. The legitimacy of war cannot be taken for granted but neither has it disappeared from the horizon.

All are agreed that the era of world peace has not yet dawned. Indeed, as Boulding says, "The instability of empire, the instability of peace and cyclical stability of war compose the constant theme of the whole age of civilization from 5000 BC to the present time".[2] There are two themes contained in the above quotation: the first, which has caught the attention of all strategic thinkers, as to why and how wars occur with unfailing regularity, and the second, which is not such an innocent obverse of the former, as to why they fail with such unceasing regularity in achieving their objects. Boulding himself notes that nothing fails like success, and one may add, in the context of the continuous resort to war, nothing succeeds like failure! There is therefore, a third philosophical question arising out of this paradox, which is: why is warfare so persistently resorted to in spite of its repeated failure to reach its goals?

However, it has been the received wisdom of humanity so far that warfare is symptomatic of power struggles between nations (or tribes, clans and other groups) and that this is a very natural state of affairs. Power struggles may be territorial, economic or religious and ideological but they are inevitable and often end in violence, as history is witness. Clausewitz, the renowned military theorist of the nineteenth century while reflecting on the phenomenon of warfare, came up with his now famous dictum, that warfare is a continuation of state policy by other means. This analysis, whatever the environment in which it was conceived, has in fact served as a very powerful legitimization of the practice of warfare amongst nation states. It may have reflected the reality of nineteenth-century European politics, but today the statement possesses normative force in a debate where the propriety of warfare has begun to be questioned.[3] It tacitly accepts the theatre of international politics as a jungle where fierce power games are proper and natural, and where the only important lesson to be learnt is how to play the game to one's best advantage. George Simmel provided a philosophical-*cum*-sociological justification for this point of view by totally accepting conflict as an integral part of the sociative process, as a necessary element in group life. The group is constituted through both conflict and co-operation. As a unity the group functions homogeneously, and only in the process of reflection do we describe two tendencies where there is in fact only one relationship.[4] Having rated conflict so positively as an aspect of unity, he took a more 'detached' view of conflict and peace, as a very natural and uninterrupted series of alternations, "Both in the succession and in the simultaneity of social life, the two are so interwoven that in every state of peace the conditions of future conflict, and in every conflict, the conditions of future peace, are formed".[5] It is merely a subjective feeling to look upon conflict as the preliminary and peace as the end of purpose of the process.

Whereas Clausewitz suggested that the parties in conflict were just individual sovereign states concerned with their national interests, other theorists have included warfare in an overall systematic view, where it is explained as part of a universal process, larger than the individual combatants through which it manifests. A grandiose systematic view was held by Hegel, in which conflict and warfare positively contributed to reaching the third leg of the dialectical triad—synthesis. Even more specifically, Hegel counted as one of the benefits of war, the firming up of the national ethos, leading to a desirably sharper national identity.[6]

Karl Marx, in his takeover and inversion of the Hegelian system, also endorsed the role of conflict and violence in the context of dialectical and historical materialism. However, he transposed the legitimacy of warfare from the international sphere, where he condemned the 'wars of the bourgeoisie', to interclass conflict, where it supposedly cut across national frontiers. Nonetheless, he saw some functional utility in the national wars of the middle classes in that at some stage, it would be possible to convert them into 'revolutionary' conflicts by turning the wrath of the ranks from the enemy of their alienated leaders. Marx did not envision warfare as inevitable for mankind, but was prepared to make use of violent conflict to bring about the emancipation and rule of the proletariat under communism, which he believed, would ultimately usher in world peace. Lenin's account of the inevitability of the wars of capitalism was but an extension of the Marxian thesis. He again, was not opposed to use violence as a means: he pleaded with his comrades for non-participation in the First World War of the capitalists, but was not squeamish in indulging in warfare and violence to consolidate state power when the opportunity presented itself.[7]

Apart from the systematisers, there are those, particularly in the aftermath of the twentieth-century wars, who accept conflict as inevitable in society, but seek for a way to isolate and contain the phenomenon of war. Some regard the military 'machine', which is bigger and more powerful than the wills of the individual decision-makers, as the inevitable cause of war. This would indicate that peace lies in the direction of reducing stockpiling and proliferation of arms and weapons systems. Those who see warfare as the result of ideological clash stress conference diplomacy and initiate or perhaps pray, for some 'maturation processes' to set in. Anatol Rapaport emphasizes the 'symbolic universe' within which human beings interact with one another, and where war reflexes may be triggered-off, perhaps even unintentionally, by the appropriate symbol. War avoidance shifts therefore to the region of manipulation of symbols.[8]

Most would probably tend to agree that war is bad, but inevitable, and therefore every state while working if possible, towards building structures for world peace, has to have a defence system in reserve to cope with any eventuality. There are many international tensions, due to economic disparities, competition, 'historical disputes and various other compulsions: hence while praying to God for peace we must keep our powder dry.

Of these there are some who believe that we are gradually moving towards a position when war will disappear from the world, in the same way, as it appears, small-pox has disappeared, or sati. Kotarbinski is one who has faith in this rational new world, and stresses the need for avoiding warfare, but not at all costs, it is important to be realistic and not be defeated if a state of war exists. Armed battle is 'a tragic necessity'.[9]

The pacifists have no use for armed warfare at all. Tolstoy and Gandhi are among those who regard war, the spectacle of humans killing humans, as a social disease. The concern of both these and their successors has been to forge non-violent methods for struggle (conflict) and to turn 'malign' fights into 'benign' ones. Mahatma Gandhi in particular, had a positively favourable view of non-violent conflicts, undertaken in particular circumstances for which he laid down the rules. Tolstoy was also favourable to non-violent struggles for justice: although he condemned internal violence or external warfare as irrational, he accepted them as inevitable choices for state policy. He was driven to an anarchist condemnation of the state, and stressed the need to meet violence with Christian love. Both Gandhi and Tolstoy rejected the inevitability of warfare, believing it to be possible to contain or transform conflict through moral and spiritual means.[10] Von Weisacker in the Politics of Peril points to the need for a 'transformation of consciousness' to achieve peacefulness.[11] In other words, he emphasizes the necessity for a transformation in human awareness and response to the symbolic universe.[12] Sri Aurobindo held similar views.

There are thus basically two types of prevalent views on the subject of conflict and war. First, that conflict is endemic to human society, so that as long as there are people in the world there will be conflicts of interests amongst them. This view produces two different responses: one, that conflict and warfare are natural and positive, serving a basic human purpose, and the task is merely to master the rules of the game to play it well and two, that conflict is inevitable but can be contained: instead of being allowed to deteriorate into malign forms of violence and warfare, it can be transformed into a benign mode. The second approach to conflict and war is that although these serve some larger logical or evolutionary purposes, the final goal of society is to be minimally without warfare and maximally without conflict. Again, there are two responses to this premise: one, that only through conflict will conflict finally be laid to rest (the Marxist-Hegelian type of dialectic), or that only through psychic transformation, through transformation of consciousness in every individual psyche, will conflict and warfare be eradicated from the world.[13]

Our approach, while sharing some of these features, is yet a different point of view from both. We certainly accept the prevalence of conflict throughout human history and also that conflict was in some way essential to the universal purpose, but not for ever conflict in today's world is mainly dysfunctional. Warfare can have only negative consequences, and non-violence is a preferable, but only intermediate stage because it still embodies a conflictual process. There is not need to accept the theory of evolution: individual centres do not 'evolve' but retain a basic identity, and in any case the interpretation of history ruled out evolution or progress and emphasized instead a see-saw pattern with periodic frustration.[14] Hence, there was no question of any natural process which would inevitably lead to a society without warfare and conflict. Conflict characterizes a stage of the universe, the third stage, and it will come to an end once this stage is over. This will involve the co-operation of all the individuals in the world, but not merely through a personal sadhana. An individual is an individual through his or her interactions, so that striving towards peaceableness must always be social as well as individual. It will involve first knowledge of the fact that conflict arises out of the human social situation which is characterized by unequal valuation and that awareness of the functioning of logic and mythology together with the practice of mutual abstention can bring an immediate halt to conflict, once that becomes the goal we set before ourselves. After this will commence the stage of imaging the new social order, an effort requiring universal co-operation, and this will be the state of harmony. It is not the final goal however, but a necessary preliminary for the new order to emerge. The new order will be one of fulfillment, the true pair of frustration, for which the logic of the universe is due to make provision.

It may be objected that if history has been characterized by conflict, co-operation is equally part of the record of the human race, and indeed, it was against this peaceful foil to the historical setting of conflict, that Gandhi had pinned his hopes on the possibility of a non-violent human society.

"It is a strange and curious phenomenon that while men and women preached peace and unity for mankind, they never could desist from waging war against considerable sections of the same mankind. While they scrupulously made professions of goodwill and peace for the whole of the human race, they sought to materialize that profession by putting to the sword millions and millions of the same race. And this happened not merely in wars that were frankly religious in the main, but also in wars that were waged on the political and economic plane. While equality, liberty and fraternity for mankind at large were proclaimed with a burning zeal, human life was held as cheap as a pumpkin whenever by chance it cast the shadow of doubt. Even today the same inscrutable phenomenon can be seen striding across the political horizon. In the wake of this almost diabolic march of peace, it has been difficult to know what is peace or who are the claimants to the heritage and pedigree of main".[15]

Notes and References

1. J.B. Kriplani, "Gandhi and Future of World Peace" in G. Ramchandran & T.K. Mahadevan (eds.) *Quest for Gandhi*, New Delhi, Gandhi Peace Foundation, 1970, p. 238.
2. Kenneth Boulding, State Peace, Texas, 1978.
3. Anatal Rapaport (ed.) Clausewitz on War, Harmands Worth, England, 1968 pp. 11-80.
4. Georg Simmel, Conflict and the Web of Group Affiliations, Illinois, 1955, p. 23.
5. *Ibid.*, p. 108.
6. W.T. Stace, The Philosophy of Hegel, New York, 1995, p. 437.
7. K. Marx, F. Engels, V. Lenin, On Historical Materialism, Moscow, 1972, pp. 520-24.
8. Anatol Rapaport, Conflict in a Man-made Environment, Harmonds Worth, England, 1974.
9. Ija Lazari Pawlowska, The Ethical Teaching of Tadeusz Kotarbinski, Dialectics and Humanism, Winter, 1977, p. 57.
10. Kuldeep Nag (ed.), Tolstoy & Gandhi, Patna, 1950, pp. 81-98.
11. Carl Fredrich Von Weizscacker, 'Politics and Consciousness', in *The Politics of Peril; Economics Society and The prevention of War*, New York, pp. 235-69.

12. Sri Aurobindo, The Human Cycle; The Idea of Human Unity, Pondicherry, 1977, pp. 582-87.
13. Madhuri Sondhi, The Making of Peace, New Delhi, Select Books, 1995, p. 193.
14. *Ibid.*
15. *Ibid.*

Role of Education in Peace Building

2

RANJAN GARG

> *"May the sky be peaceful, land peace giving, may the mind be peaceful, may the earth be peaceful, may the water be peaceful, may the plants be peaceful, may the forest be peaceful, may all the bounties of nature be peaceful, may there be peace and peace only, may such a peace come to all.*
>
> (Yajur Veda xxv1.17)

In the last few decades the world has witnessed increase in conflicts- interstate, intrastate, intercommunity, intra-community and so on. The increasing number of conflicts and its negative impact on the quality of life and development of nation and community has made it clear that through war and conflicts goals of peace and prosperity can never be attained. The parties involved in the conflicts (powerful or powerless) actually both are sufferers. This indicates that to see victory in the war as achievement is merely a myth as war can never lead us to achievement of peace and prosperity.

The negative relation between violent conflicts and social prosperity and social good has compelled the social scientists to search for an alternative paradigm. Emergence of peace studies is a step in the direction of search for such an alternative. It has also been realized that only elimination of visible forms of conflicts cannot established a peaceful society. What required is to abolish the vary roots of conflicts. It has been realized that the sustainable peace can be obtained only through inculcation of peaceful values and peace education.

The notion of peace is one of the most ambiguous concepts having multiple meanings. In broad terms the notion of peace can be divided into negative peace and positive peace. The notion of negative peace considers peace merely as the end or absence of widespread violent conflicts associated with war. If seen from this perspective even the society in which social violence and structural violence are prevalent can be labeled as a peaceful society. In contradictions to this limited notion of peace, the concept of positive peace established that the goal of peace cannot be achieve only by eliminating the visible forms of violence rather what required is removable of the major potential causes of future conflicts. If seen from this perspective only a just and fair society is fit to be addressed as a peaceful society. Some of the significant features of such a society can be enumerated as follow:

- An active and egalitarian civil society.
- Inclusive democratic and non violent structures and processes.
- An open and accountable government

The notion of positive peace enlarges the scope of peace building. It includes the promotion and encouragement of new forms of citizenship and political participation to develop active democracies. So peace building can be seen as an activity that leads to the elimination of lethal and traumatizing conflicts by just provision of resources for individual survival through group activities based on social justice. To illustrate, Christie emphasizes the satisfaction of human needs as structural peace building. U.N. Secretary-general Boutros Ghali has defined peace building as 'action to identify and support structures which will tend to strengthen and solidify peace in order to relapse into conflict'. [B.B. Ghali, An Agenda for Peace, Preventive Diplomacy, Peacemaking and Peace Keeping, Report of the Secretary-General Pursuant to the Statement adopted by the Summit Meeting of the Security Council on 31 January 1992, UN Doc A/47/277-S/24111, 17 June 1992, Para 21].

Some of important peace building measures, according to Ghali are disarmament, restoring order, the custody and possible destruction of weapons repatriation of refugees, support for security personnel, education monitoring of governmental institutions and promoting formal and informal processes of political participation. In the same manner, UN Secretary General Kofi Annan emphasized on the need of re-integration and resumed development. [See, Kofi Annan, The causes of conflict and the Promotion of Durable Peace in Africa, Report of the Secretary-General to the U.N. Security Council, UN Doc A/52/871-S/1998/318, 16 April 1998, Para 63].

Thus, the broader notion of peace building encompasses socio-political and economic reconstruction of society, establishment of constitutional, administrative and legal structures and determination of resource allocation. In addition to it, physical reconstruction of a society viz., houses, roads, schools, electricity, hospitals and other infrastructure. But all these efforts in the direction of peace-building would fail in yielding required result in the absence of creation of positive value system and culture of peace through which only peace centric values can be inculcated and transmitted from one generation to other generation.

Only through creation of culture of the peace the possibility of re-emergence of traumatizing conflicts can be minimized. The question arises how the goal of culture of peace can be built? Here comes the significant role of education in promoting the culture of peace. If peace-building aims at reconstruction of the society, (physical, economic, social, psychological) then what can be the better means to such a reconstruction than education? The next question that arises is what kind of education can play a positive role in the process of peace building?

Peace education is an essential component of quality basic education. Peace education is a process of promoting the knowledge, skills, attitudes and values needed to bring about behavioral changes that will enable pupils and younger generations at educational institutions to prevent conflicts and violence or solve their conflicts in a peaceful manner, whether it is at interpersonal, intrapersonal, intergroup, intra-group, national or international level.

Peace is not an academic inquiry or an intelligence discipline alone, it is rather an approach or an outlook or a way to lead the life. Its responsibility is to rebuild the broken man by offering him internal peace and restoring the devasted society and promoting the external peace. Peace education is pedagogical efforts to create a better world.

AIMS OF PEACE EDUCATION

- To understand the nature and origins of violence and its effects.
- To create environment for achieving peaceful society.
- To be aware of various conflicts at different levels.
- To investigate the causes of conflicts.
- To encourage various skills to end the conflicts in a peaceful manner.
- To be equipped with various conflict resolution techniques.

Education serves as a vehicle for culture and values and creates an environment where socialization can take place. The schools, colleges and universities are the formal agencies established by society to shape personality of younger generation in a way that they will prove useful members to the society. Various social problems and violence shown on media cannot be left behind at school gates. Schools have to play a vital role not only in identifying these problems, but also to develop the ability among students to see the implications of their behaviors and channelize their energies in positive and constructive direction.

UNESCO has identified 15 symptoms of intolerance for both elementary and secondary level students. To point out a few of them: (1) language used by students, (2) stereotyping, (3) teasing, (4) prejudices, (5) scapegoat, (6) misconduct, (7) discrimination, (8) harassment and bullying.

Bullying is the most common problem witnessed in schools and colleges. This is major challenges for teachers how to handle students? Teaching for peace calls for emphasizing both the cognitive and affective domain of personality and adopting strategies of teaching according to the need and requirements of the topic and level of the students.

Education can promote peace by following methods:

1. *Cooperative Learning*: It encourages an interactive form of learning that enables children to deal with complexity of life and be confident. Children will learn to discharge the social responsibility with more commitment and confidence. It will improve interpersonal relationship. Group based activities should be encouraged.

2. *Story Telling*: This method can be adopted by teachers to teach peace, tolerance, human rights, etc. various historical events and their implication on peace and human rights may be narrated to children.
3. *Conflict Resolution*: Conflicts in society are inevitable. We adopt our strategy to resolve the conflicts. Results may vary from constructive to destructive. Children should be trained to resolve their conflicts through non-violent and cooperative methods. A culture of peace will develop when members of society learn to resolve their difference amicably. Today children's aggressive behavior can be witnessed everywhere in class, playground, roads and canteen etc. schools need to monitor and channelized these conflicts in constructive direction. If they are left unchannelized, they may pose serious threat to society.
4. *Transpersonal Strategies*: Peace education also means deep self analysis. It can be encouraged by meditation, yoga and games. These have been recognized as a powerful technique to reduce conflicts and tensions and control aggressive behavior and increase concentration. There are many more methods which demand our concern. Parent-teacher meetings at school can provide a big platform for peace education among children.
5. *Social Service Camp*: These camps can be organized in areas where peace has been disturbed by violence or terrorism. Students should be made aware of consequences of violence.
6. *Dramatics and literary Activities*: Student can be motivated to carry out activities related to peace issues. Violence and terrorism can be dramatized to sensitize students against them.
7. *Role of Teachers*: Teachers can play a major role in peace building education. Teachers should be the role model for their students. Teachers themselves try to solve the various problems of educational institution with non-violent means. They should not promote violence of any kind in educational system.
8. *Development of the Peace Consciousness*: Efforts can be made to keep violence in outside any form from the

institution. Necessary atmosphere in the institution should be developed to promote peace education. School and colleges should not indulge in any violent activity rather difference should be solved peacefully by peaceful means.

9. *Inter Religious Experiences*: Education institution can provide students religious experiences that belong to the different religious. Efforts should be based especially on the prayers functions and ceremonies that have a universal significance on the members of other religious communities.
10. *Peace Literature and Events*: contemporary children's literature can be used to raise discussion about issues of peace and conflicts. Encourage students to come up with their own Solutions to conflicts: How to resolve the conflicts can be taught through stories or carbons characters.

The books like, I am Malala by Malala Yousafzi, Weidenfeld & Nicolson, London (youngest Peace Noble Prize Awardee) can be used to tell the younger generation how horrible can the conflicts be and how they destabilize the human personality this book has inspired many children to take action against violence. Artwork can also promote the cultural of peace among the students. Children can be encouraged to produce their own artwork on peace and violence. It can be in the form of stories, poems, songs, drawings on the theme of peace.

It is important to remember that peace education can be introduce as an additional academic subject we add to the existing disciplines or can also be the general orientation that we can introduce in existing subjects. Economics and sociology can teach peaceful co-existence as well as peaceful development. Science text books can teach the need to fight for ban on nuclear weapons of mass destruction and international agreement on it. Biology can teach deadly effects of exposure of radioactivity on human beings. Political Science can teach the aftereffects of wars to human beings. The challenge for educators all over the globe is to choose between going ahead with present education system or preparing our younger generation for the life that is peaceful, secure, spiritually beautiful and materially affluent.

CURRICULUM FOR PEACE EDUCATION

Education can be a tool of peace building but for that complete overhaul of education system is required. Education for peace requires appropriate training for the teachers. Only then they would be able to effectively participate in education for peace.

Education can play contributory role in peace building but for that some new addition in the curriculum is required. In fact, alternative curriculum needs to be developed for peace education. On the basis of our interviews with the peace researchers and educationists we have reached the conclusion that following model of curriculum can be adopted for peace education.

Primary School

At the primary school level the curriculum should include stories, poems and dramas based on spiritual and moral values. Stories from different religious, regions and countries should also be taught to the students so that they can know about different ways of life and can also accept them.

Middle School

At the level of middle school, the students should be taught the life sketch and peace initiatives of the leaders like Gandhi, Nehru, Vinoba Bhave, Mother Taresa, Nelson Mandela, Martin Luther and Tagore, etc.

High School

At this level an attempt should be made to give conceptual understanding about peace to the students. Therefore, high school curriculum should include concept of peace, areas of peace, means to achievement of peace, different philosophers on world peace; peace imitative by UN, UNESCO, Red Cross Society, YMCA, etc. In addition to it, students should also be made aware of the consequences of war and violence.

HIGHER EDUCATION

At this level, a number of changes and additions have been made in the curriculum. A number of Universities, offer UGC sponsored M.Phil and Ph.D. courses in peace studies. Peace centers have also been established as teaching and research centers which organize workshops and seminars in peace studies and through it impart practical peacemaking skills to the students. Further, through engaging the students in different peace projects, these centers help students to deal with the real in situations in field and managing them.

Both the peace researchers and educationists accept that some of the above referred measures have been implemented in practice and have also been proved successful. But still, miles to go, as there are certain obstacles in the path of peace education, to name few of them:

- Inadequate allocation of funds.
- Lack of encouragement from the government.
- Age old traditional values related to violence, war and power.
- Erosion of traditional moral values related to peace, love and humanism.
- Predominant individualism and capitalist attitude.
- Ethnic divide, religious narrow mindedness, poverty, unemployment and under development.

CONCLUSION

Despite the above referred obstacles peace education can play a very significant role in sustaining the process of peace building. There is an urgent need to make the education system sensitive to accommodate the needs to fall the communities and inclusive. It should be able to develop critical and analytical thinking and empathy in students. Peace should not be considered as merely a moral value rather should be seen as a skill for survival which would enable people to live in harmony and peace. To sum up, peace education can be one of the best ways to take away an individual, group of individuals or the society as a whole from the path of violence and promote tolerance. Thus, the students should be trained in peace through peace tours, peace rallies, peace exhibition, celebration of peace festivals, etc.

The way we have created the 'culture of violence' in the same way we have to create 'a culture of peace' among our younger generation.

References

Ashu Pasricha (ed.)' "Gandhi in 20th Century", Article by Ranjan Garg, "Peace Education: Action & Refection Deep & Deep Publications, New Delhi, 2011.

Balwinder Kaur, "Peace Education, New Trends & Innovations", Deep & Deep Publications, Pvt. Ltd, New Delhi, 2006.

Balwinder Kaur, "Teaching of Peace and Conflict Resolution, New Trends & Innovations", Deep & Deep Publications, Delhi, 2006.

Poonam Bawa and H.S. Rathore, "Gandhian Concept of Basic Education Saviour of Modern India", in Journal of Gandhian Studies, Vol. VIII, No. 1, 2010.

Ranjan Garg, "Peace and Security. In Search of a New Paradigm", Regal, Publications, New Delhi, 2012.

S.P. Uday Kumar, "Peace Education in India: A Proposal" in South Asia *Journal of Peace Building,* Vol. 2, No. 1, autumn, 2009.

UNESCO (2001) Learning the Way of Peace: A Teachers' Guide to Peace Education.

UNESCO (1994), UNESCO culture of peace progrmmes. Teaching for Peace and Peace Curriculum in Manipur, Eastern Social Research Centre, Manipur, 2012.

Education for Peace

3

HARDARSHAN KAUR

Violence is emerging in an unprecedented manner in human society. Looking at the world today any sensible person looks disheartened and even horrified to see the kind of violent acts being committed by man against man and nature. It is very sad to document that we are living in an era of unprecedented violence in the form of terrorism, war, crimes, injustice, oppression and exploitation amidst a seemingly outward development enjoyed by a few. The majority of mankind lives in stark poverty, struggling for bare survival and is in constant chagrin. There is much disorder and confusion in the society man has built for himself. It is not possible to provide fundamental human rights, social justice, democracy, literacy, respect and dignity for all, international solidarity, respect for worker's rights, children's rights, equality between men and women, cultural identity, and diversity, indigenous peoples' and minorities' rights, preservation of natural environment to name some of the obvious areas without ensuring a culture of peace and non-violence.

WHAT IS MEANT BY PEACE?

Peace may be defined as absence of war or violence in a mutually beneficial harmonious relationship among relevant parties i.e among individuals, groups or countries. World peace is an ideal of freedom, peace and happiness among and within all nations and/ or people. World peace is an idea of planetary non-violence by which nations willingly co-operate. It refers to and aims at the cessation of all hostilities and to restore conflicts without war. This definition of peace implies that peace is a relationship variable and not a trait or predisposition in an individual ,group or nation. As a relationship peace can not be maintained by separation, isolation or building barriers between conflicting parties all of which may temporarily reduce violence but will not establish the relationship required for long term peace. On the other hand if relationship is characterised by co-operation, mutual benefit, justice and respect peace is assumed to exist.

Now the question arises how can we maintain peace? I would like to quote from UNESCO preamble:

> "Since wars start in the minds of men it is in the minds of men that defence of peace must be constructed".

There is no other tool as potent as education that can change the minds of men and cultivate the culture of peace. It is a key to uniting nations, bringing closely together the warring groups. Education teaches the art of living *and* there is no better way of living than living peacefully. The world at present is plagued by racist and fundamentalist violence and the best antidote for all this is promoting education for peace and intellectual learning. Education is a key tool in combating poverty, in promoting peace, social justice, human rights and democracy, cultural diversity and environmental awareness. It is not possible to provide fundamental human rights, social justice, democracy, literacy, respect and dignity for all, international solidarity, respect for workers' rights, children's rights, equality between men and women, cultural identity and diversity, indigenous peoples' and minorities' rights, the preservation of natural environment to name some of the obvious thematics without ensuring a culture of peace and non-violence.

EDUCATION FOR PEACE

Peace education is the process of promoting the knowledge, skills, attitudes and values needed to bring about behaviour changes that will enable children, youth and adults to prevent conflict and violence both overt and structural; to resolve conflict peacefully; and to create conditions conducive to peace, whether at intrapersonal, interpersonal, intergroup, national or international level.

Education for peace implies—Teaching the information, attitudes, values and behaviour competencies needed to resolve conflicts without violence and to build and maintain mutually beneficial and harmonious relationships. It implies concept of peace through values, life skills and knowledge in a spirit of equality, respect, empathy, understanding and mutual appreciation among individuals and nations.

The ultimate goal of peace education is two fold :

- Making the person at peace with himself, i.e inner peace.
- Enabling the person to establish peace with the outside world.

Inner Peace

Discovering inner peace is concerned with the resolution of one's own psychological conflicts and problems and taming one's own mind by relegating unconditionally to cosmic power. A person who is at peace with himself blossoms from within and makes his surroundings peaceful and fragrant. A person happy and content from within radiates positive waves, accepts other fellow beings with an open mind. Only such a person can have a feeling of universal brotherhood. For him in the words of The Holy Guru Granth Sahib:

> Neither anybody is a foe nor unrelated. Everybody is a friend.
>
> and
>
> I have befriended every one and I am related to every body.

This is a stage of inner peace or ecstasy and attained only with God's grace. There is no other way than spiritual education for helping the individual to attain inner peace. Spiritual education has to be through practical religion which should inculcate the humanistic values in the children. In the most easily comprehensible The Holy Granth, like other religious scriptures the concepts of universal brotherhood, fellow feeling, oneness of mankind irrespective of social cultural and economic status have been emphasised which are basic tenets on which the edifice of world peace can be built. Guru Nanak stressed the need to balance work, worship and charity and defending the rights of all fellow human beings to attain the state of optimistic resilience. Spiritual education can help the individual by making the person understand himself, his origin and his ultimate destiny so that he does not enter mad race for material possessions, sheds his inflated ego and imbibes divine qualities of forgiveness and sacrifice for the welfare of the whole mankind at the same time remaining content with his earnings through honest means. He does not feel jealous of others possessions and achievements but remains satisfied with his own fortunes.

Peace with the Outside World

Man is a social animal and can't have inner peace in isolation. Even the prophets could not remain aloof from social upheavals and fought wars against injustice and oppression. To be at peace with outside world a feeling of equality, sharing, helping, no hatred towards anyone, tolerance, forgiveness and cooperation is required to be developed.

STRATEGIES FOR PEACE EDUCATION

Exploring the Root Cause of Conflict

Negative emotions like anger, jealousy, lust, hatred and pride are the root cause of racist and fundamentalist violence in the world and the best solution is providing education for peace and intellectual learning.

Dismantling the Culture of War and Violence

This is concerned with mitigating all support for war system including competitive games, gender oppression, banning toys promoting violence and teaching children destructive behaviours like toy guns, knives, violent video games and violence in films.

Understanding of Human Rights

Making the children understand equality and justice in civil, economic, political, cultural and religious rights for all communities and making them feel that all castes, creeds and races are equal. Discrimination on the basis of caste, creed and socio-economic status needs to be snubbed.

Conflict Management

Passive coexistence is not a viable path to maintain peace. Peace does not mean absence of conflicts. Conflicts do occur and it is not avoidance, suppression or denial of differences that maintain peace, but facing conflicts as they occur and resolving them constructively on the basis of consensus and not by oppression.

Global Disarmament

This includes pruning budget on security, dismantling the already amassed nuclear, chemical and biological weapons, stopping/curtailing their further proliferation and redirecting the fund allocation towards sustainable development.

Role of School

The strategy for promoting the concept of world peace concerns the content of education and training, educational resources and materials, school and community life, training of teachers and research. A culture of peace must take roots in the classroom at an early age. It must continue to be reflected in curriculum at the secondary and tertiary levels. Educators should be aware of the direct and indirect forms of violence and the war system so as to overcome those.

Active listening, dialogue, mediation, cooperative learning for providing understanding and respect for universal values and rights needs to be cultivated. It requires participation at all levels i.e family, school, places of work, play grounds and other community as well as other forums. Education for peace must be trans-disciplinary, included in all learning spaces and not limited to a single classroom or subject. The learning spaces should foster intercultural and international dialogue and respect knowledge of national and global systems of governance, respect for life and commitment to non-violence.

Schools can contribute towards world peace in many ways, i.e through Curriculum, methods of teaching, co-curricular activities some of which are enumerated below:

- Help students develop inner peace through activities like yoga and devotional music.
- Curriculum should focus on social rather than individual issues.
- Subjects included should develop interdependence between communities and nations.
- Teaching for human rights should be included with the aim of promoting among all human beings the spirit of understanding, tolerance and peaceful coexistence to

stimulate cooperation among people and to help them lesson obstacles to world peace and progress.

- Educators can use cooperative games, participative pedagogy and creative problem solving activities that emphasize learning to work and live together.
- Develop a more humanistic management approach. Students can play participatory role in the school affairs.
- Classroom environment should be democratic, participative rather than authoritarian.
- The teachers should not allow one or a few students to dominate the class time silencing majority. They should rather provide equal opportunities to all students irrespective of religion, caste, creed and socio-economic and educational status of parents and shun favouritism which breeds jealousy and hatred which is the main cause of crime among students today.
- discouraging/avoiding derogatory racial remarks/ writings.
- Revision of History books should be done in such a way that atrocities committed in the past are not unnecessarily highlighted which may instigate revenge. Efforts should be made to undo the damage and start afresh.
- Civic education projects can be undertaken in which classroom teaching can be combined with community service to promote civic responsibility among youth and prepare them for active citizenship.
- Our schools though wanting to develop democratic values and community inter-dependence, end up developing capitalistic and individualistic values through competitive activities that breed greed and exclusion. This needs to be replaced by strategies like cooperative learning where collective achievement of the group is more important than individual achievement.
- Improve human relations between
  teacher-student
  teacher-teacher
  student-student

By developing attitudes of mutual respect and cooperation in students and teachers and making them emotionally and socially mature rather than egoistic and self centred .

References

Dewey, J., 1916, Education and democracy, New York: Free Press.

Galtung, J., 1969, Violence, peace and peace research. *Journal of Peace Research*, 6(3): 167-91.

Galtung, J., 1996, Peace by peaceful means: Peace and conflict and civilization. London: Sage Publications.

Montessori, M., 1949, Education for peace. Oxford, England: CLIO, 1995.

UN General Assembly, 1997, International year for a culture of peace, 2000. A/RES/52/15.

UN General Assembly, 1998, Declaration on a culture of Peace. A/RES/53/243A.

The Ethics of Non-Violence, Peace and Security

4

KIRAN CHAUHAN

From across the waters, the single image of India in myriad minds is that of the modern saint-in-action, Mahatma Gandhi. As unmistakably Indian as the Vedic hymns or the high Himalayas, he yet represents the simplest villager-traditionally kind, hard-working and long-suffering but now touched by a new orld dynamism which Gandhi himself brought to his people. When he took to the road, harnessed himself to the service of truth and freedom, India rediscovered its inheritance but also confronted the issues of a larger interdependence. Surprised, the powerful nations saw the power of an irresistible moral personality, owning nothing, unarmed but working through the aroused will of millions. Equally ranged against apathy and discrimination at the home front as he was against exploitation from outside, the intrepid leader gave a new meaning to modern nationalism which needs a wider human context even for its own survival. "The matchless weapon", as he called it, of revolution without violence brought results unparallelled in our age. Austere, tender and accessible to all, Gandhi was spiritually enmeshed in a detailed concern for his fellow-beings; his Truth-force or Satyagraha was an enormous readjustive strength which was applied in simultaneous action at basic levels. The freedom movement under his guidance moved into farms and industries, helped in resolving communal and political disputes, and brought a new urgency in planning for health, education and religious enlightenment. Opposing evil at each point he also initiated remedial changes instead of further inflaming and destroying relationships. And yet he carried his burden lightly like an artist-ascetic, with unfailing Aumour and a "spiritual gaiety" that balanced his servere self-discipline. Africa, Great Britain, then India became conscious of an intriguing figure, till gradually the greater part of mankind knew of a mature, benign leader of history who worked for the larger freedom of which political freedom was a part.[1]

And in a blaze of glory he left, martyred in a prayer meeting, his palms join in mercy, the name of god on his lips.

Who was Mahatma Gandhi? How can we assess him? He is evidently too near for us to raise our eyes in vertical measurement which, in any case, will be unattainable. As a profoundly religious man, Gandhi was the supreme humanist in the modern crisis. Obviously not a man of science or art in the conventional sense, he used his techniques as precision instruments in what he called "Experiments with Truth", while the relevant purpose, control and design invested his life work with high artistry. To this he added a mystique of faith that took account of the entire human situation. No wonder that a poet lilke Tagore and a scientist such as Einstein acclaimed his arrival as the great event, that religious men in far removed disciplines felt equally moved by his witness. Hence, the further paradox that artists, writers playwrights and we have mentioned the world of science were drawn to him from their own constellations to celebrate an alien star whose brightness they recognized. Bernard Shaw, luckily, was known by name to Gandhi, so their encounter did not surprise the Indian saint; but in the case of Charlie Chaplin, Gandhi's completely innocent ignorance all the more endeared him to the great artist comedian. Romain Rolland's chronicle of his discussions with Gandhi in Geneva, and his well-known book, led to a chain of new West-East alignments and loyalties that continues.[2]

Another fact of Gandhi's relationship with creative art should be mentioned. Wherever Gandhi went, song and festival, prayer meetings and Yatras followed him; he could not have endured what he did without his reciprocative joy in this resurgence. He rejoiced in Tagore's poetry; he knew and admired port Vallathol whose name is now a household word all over India; he warmly recognized the art of Nandalal Bose, the great painter. Abroad, he marveled at some of the Western architectural masterpieces, for instance, in the universally beloved London; a city he knew well. His response to music was immediate and profound. Gandhi, as we know, accepted the purest flower of Indian music in Subbulakshmi's songs, songs which have now spread beauty and devotion to far shores beyond India. Bhajans, Christian hymns, chants from the Quran were a part of his daily evening worship. The lonely pilgrim, stick in hand, crossing a frail bamboo bridge in Noakhali had time to halt and listen to Ramlila in a broken village; he delighted in and regenerated rural crafts and regional cultures. One saw him look deeply into the village sky and the riverine scene at sunset as he walked the long stretch. Above all, his eyes would light up at the sight of children, he blessed the homes and families wherever he stopped for a moment of talk or for shelter. Evidently this was a new type of revolutionary leader, strongly modern and yet immediately recognizable as belonging to a more inclusive world history.[3]

Again, do we know Gandhi? Hardly, A man of sorrows who had a word of cheer, who went to flaming villages and put out the fire of hatred, who taught us to love each other as Hindus, Muslims, Christians and others, who mightily fought against drug addiction, priestcraft, landlordism, foreign or indigenous oppression, and yet seemed to be in active rest while the storm raged. Awake at dawn in prayer, hard at work till late hours, leading thousands of people all over the land, this man could laugh at himself as he would laugh at fear or death. Willing to sell his Mahatmaship at an auction sale—that was as much as he cared for this attribution by friends—if he could raise funds for the needy, at home in all religions when the practitioners were good men; yet he belonged to his own particular inheritance of faith which grew with his own experiences. Opposed to machines and mechanization he yet stirred villagers towards ceaseless new experiments and broke their fixation to usages they had outlived; he even fell under the lure of electricity in Lyons in France when he saw that new power could be tamed and used by lace makers in their own homes instead of the families being uprooted and thrown into ganglionic city slums. Being assured of his complete identification with India he did not idolize India or inculate geolatry which attributed all virtues to one land and excluded it from others. The earth was a fair place for him, where he lived at home, though home for him was where India suffered and strove to recover its life.

Mahatma Gandhi was never a crusader for peace so much as a non-violent warrior in the cause of justice. Again and again he declared himself to be against the 'peace of the grave'. As a fighter he was engaged in a battle to destroy peace, the deathly peace of the Pax Britannica, and through fanning the flames of dissatisfaction and 'divine discontent' amongst his own people, he succeeded in provoking the British Government into committing ruthless acts of violence and carnage which fairly rent the veil of peace in twain.[4]

Why then has the mantle of peace been thrust upon him? Peace or 'shanti' was never a top favourite in the Mahatma's vocabulary. It was Tagore who named his university Shantiniketan and strove for an international harmony of cultures. Gandhi's ashram was called Sevagram, from service, and his other favourite concepts were satyagraha, truthful or disciplined struggle, and of course ahimsa, non-violence-both tolls of an activist who had undertaken the task of fighting for freedom and justice. He never set himself a programme for achieving world peace, although within a general evolutionary framework, he regarded India's non-violent achievement of her sovereignty as a step in that direction.[5] He abhorred war, and generally advocated non-violent means to resist the aggressor- a position which he did not abandon throughout the course of the Second World War. He did not, however, proffer any advice on how violent conflagrations are to be avoided. Ahimsa is a way of avoiding or preventing the escalation of physical violence, but is not by itself a sufficient condition for establishing peace, if by peace is meant absence of conflict. In fact Gandhi followed the conventional assumption, that peace could only be achieved in the aftermath of justice: his own unique contribution was to struggle for justice non-violently. But non-violence and peace are by no means the same thing. However, hope of eliciting willy-nilly from the Mahatma a Gandhian peace programme has not yet been totally abandoned.

It has been suggested for instance, that India's policy of non-alignment was a step in the direction or world peace-part of her Gandhian legacy. Non-alignment might just be interpreted methodologically as an extension of ahimsa, if we wished to stretch a point, in so far as it initially entailed non-involvement in armed conflict and military pacts, and could thereby be said to be resisting super power conflict through 'non-cooperation'. However, this policy was not born out of a dispassionate global outlook, but was based purely on self-interest in the context of a world order whose justice or injustice. India did not wish to challenge. Being an international satyagraha was not considered a feasible foreign policy role, so India made the required change from a position of rectitude that would have demanded justice and freedom for all, to a stand-off role for herself. (Of course, she has continued on a selective basis to champion the rights of the exploited and the unfree, but not universally). India was prepared now to work for peace, at an international level with honour and justice where possible, but was also ready for compromise where the dictates of expediency demanded. Thus she violated one of the fundamentals of the Gandhian position even while continuing to use the rhetoric of non-violence: but even that suffered an ignoble demise when the Indian troops marched in to liberate Goa (to facilitate the winning of a parliamentary bye-election).

As Gandhi had predicted, the disgust with war, particularly after the atomic bombings in Japan, did not last ("...the world will return to violence with renewed zeal after the disgust is worn out") and the post-war international environment collapsed with the West European-Egyptian clash over the Suez Canal. With the public return of realpolitik in national and international politics, the use of Gandhian terminology becomes less and less credible and today it is the mutually unacceptable destructive capability of the nuclear arsenal that maintains a precarious balance of superpower stand-off, not peace. Local wars and violence have never ceased, not surprisingly, seeing that there is preposterously little justice or equality for the newly liberated millions in the decolonized world. For those who do not care for the dubious results of the Marxian panacea, or the rapacious other face of capitalism, still somewhere the Gandhian dream lingers on. Gandhi is studies, quantified, computerized, structurally analyzed, categorized—the desperate search is on for the buried formula in the life of that Grand Old Man—some formula that can be usefully tapped and universally applied, in international, political and even economic affairs.

This is in spite of the fact that to all appearances Gandhi in his own life failed to bring to a successful conclusion his own formula of non-violence. Could there be some very glaring fact that is staring us in the face which habitual perceptions prevent us from seeing, so that we make a virtue out of redoubling our energies in the face of failure?

THE ETHICS OF NON-VIOLENCE, JUSTICE AND PEACE

Gandhi's aim of achieving independence for India through the means of non-violent satyagraha is the cornerstone of his claim to be apolitical moralist, or ethical politician. If the goal of independence was the winning of human dignity for the millions of subject Indians, then this human dignity was endangered if political freedom were to be attained by violent means—violence being always a brutalising process. No matter what the history and provocation of British rule, he condemned any violent reply as intrinsically wrong. Furthermore, Gandhi shared the same faith which Vivekananda had expressed in ringing terms before him, [6] a faith in the innate dignity and divinity of all human nature, and he essayed always to appeal to the 'best' in his adversary, to bring about a moral conversion in the other, so that the latter's eyes would be opened to the justice and truth of the satyagrahi's cause, and he would thereby be moved to accede to his demands.

Gandhi's thoughts and actions flowed from his principle of satyagraha. In so far as it means abiding in truth, or holding on to truth, it is a much wider concept than mere passive resistance. In fact it ceases to be just a means to an end; the end of human activity is already implicit as 'truth' in satyagraha, and the means to be adopted to arrive at the truth are to be such as facilitate reaching the required goal.

However, the problem arises with defining truth; Gandhi, although believing truth to be an absolute value, was aware that no human can claim to have an absolute knowledge of it. Individuals have their personal understandings of truth, according to their capacities and level of evolution: the same goes for collectivities. Not being able to know unmistakably the whole truth is not a cause for inaction, however, for as moral beings we must act according to whatever insights we have remaining receptive always, to the possibility of encountering fuller or higher truths, or new facts which may alter our assessments of certain situations. In fact one may say that with Gandhi, the moral imperative was the only 'absolute', Kant had visualized the possibility of 'universalizing' the categorical imperative, but Gandhi was more aware of the relativity of truth perceptions, and confined himself to the absolute and universal need to act morally. Hence, the means became more important than the ends, and thus the importance of non-violent action. One way say that it is a Gandhian dictum that we are morally obliged to resist evil. More specifically we are morally obliged to resist social and political injustice, to act whenever we perceive an injustice, we believe we are in the right, but there is always a possibility that we may not see the whole truth, that the oppressor whom we are resisting may be partially or even wholly in the right. Thus it becomes imperative to keep up a dialogue with him, a moral dialogue, pointing out him his injustice, and willing always to hear his point of view. It is often said that a satyagraha aims at arriving not so much at a victory, as at a settlement. In this context: the way is left open for dialogue, the moral issues do not get obscured in hatred and violence. The possibility of mutual trust arises, tactical flexibility is much greater so that responses can be adapted to the oppressor's concessions or his counter-moral appeals any total or radical confrontation is counter-productive within such a framework of understanding.[7] Satyagraha ideally should be a type of cybernetic process, groping towards truth and justice, and hence permitting a certain level of disturbance but not a total destruction, of the field of enquiry.

However, satyagraha is not merely expressed in resistance to injustice. It is a way of life for the individual as well as for the community, and thus influences the daily life and goals of the satyagraha. He is obliged to practice self-restraint and discipline. Gandhi specifically recommended chastity for understanding and strengthening the will to pursue truth. The spread of satyagraha in the community inevitably involves social reconstruction and education in all their aspects.

It has been assumed all along that perpetrators of injustice do not respond merely to moral appeals. Some action has to be initiated which forces them to act or react. Gandhi often described satyagraha as 'soul-force', a force which is ultimately more effective than mere brute or physical force. In the arena of moral dialectics therefore, he understood the importance of force, although he had his apologists have often been delicate about admitting to the use of any form of compulsion.[8] There may be an equivocation here, although a necessary one, given the open-ended and incomplete nature of the Gandhian belief-system.

The only space where fully free and voluntary dialogue about morals and justice can take place, is the debating hall, and it is superfluous to add that it does not directly lead to social change, although it may remotely affect it, once channeled through the appropriate political or executive agencies. Now Mahatma Gandhi was above all an activist, not an academic, and he was constrained to search for some form of force to achieve his goals. But given his open-ended belief system, and the non-violent techniques he adopted to permit some 'play' in the field of less-than-absolute truths, he insisted that he was not using coercion on his opponents, but wanted at best to convert them. The difficulty in this theory of non-coercion, is of course, that one party to the exercise is not a voluntary participant: he has been coerced into rethinking his situation by the non-violent provocations of the other, without which he was otherwise quite satisfied. With this amount of coercion no doubt Gandhi would go along, as did Socrates when he confessed to being the 'gadfly' which aroused the Athenians out of their complacent torpor. However, it is in the pitch at which non-violent resistance is conducted in practice, and in the actual responses and reactions that in fact take place, that the door is indeed left open for the charge of coercion, if charge it be in this context. For instance, when Gandhi made it his aim to demonstrate to the British the untenability of their rule in India if the common Indian withdrew his acquiescence or legitimacy from it, did he convert the Englishman to the view that his rule was immoral or that it was impossible in the view that his rule was immoral or that it was impossible in the new circumstances? And if a few were aware of the immorality would they have withdrawn if the possibility of continuing in the same way still existed?

Again the charge of moral blackmail is rejected with horror by the Gandhian—but what else is a fast unto death? Gandhi always regarded suffering as important for individual ascesis; he also recognized its effect on the adversary-arousing either the latter's compassion or moral revulsion at infliction of suffering on a non-resisting satyagraha. Were the adversary to concede on these grounds, it is again not necessarily a case of moral conversion: he may continue to disagree over the rights and wrongs of the matter under dispute, but capitulate due to the unbearable stress brought to bear on his own moral nature at the voluntarily courted suffering of the satyagrahis. Aware of the possibilities of misuse. Gandhi had insisted that satyagraha be used only in cases of a grave and serious nature. However, he could not help but skate the thin ice between idealism and realism.

As an idealist he wished to convert his opponent to a shared view of truth: as an activist he had to use methods which 'worked'. Since his ideal was in a sense unattainable (perfect truth), he tried to evolve a method which would be guided by a law of moral or truthful uncertainty and yet be effective in producing results. He trusted that ahimsa, carried to the point of self-suffering, would provide the insurance against mistakes, in that the ordeal would act as a restraint on the irresponsible caprices of the human intellect or spirit. However this attempt to bridge the gap between theory and practice is not without its inner contradictions and ambiguities. In fact the biggest paradox at the heart of satyagraha is, that there is no guarantee at all that the truth will always triumph-no guarantee from the nature and practice of satyagraha. Not only may the winning party be mistaken and the losing party right: both parties may be respectively mistaken, or both participate in the same illusion. Hence it is that satyagraha can only come into its own when used by one of the adversaries—preferably both—of some moral standing. Otherwise it does not manage to get off the ground.

Satyagraha and ahimsa turn out to be therefore fundamental techniques or method adopted in pursuit of social reconstruction and justice. Given the human condition, they are the best possible means for a man of conscience to follow. But does this practice of the ethics of non-violence answer the contemporary need for peace?

Gandhi was no biblical 'passivist', turning the other cheek: rather he preferred to take the initiative in thrusting forward his cheek before oppressive symbols of authority. While doing so he managed to remain quite peaceful in his own behavior, but the results of his actions were hardly pacific: his was a triumph for individual morality, forcing a breakdown in the adversary's peace-keeping arrangements, in order to highlight the latter's injustices. His demands were couched in moralistic language: he demanded moral conversion from his antagonist, although at the practical level he was content with political capitulation. But if his demands were not conceded, he threatened violence: not to the adversary, but threatened him with having to commit violence against himself or his followers. Sometimes he even had recourse to the ultimate in this form of violence-suicide-by the slow and attenuating process of a fast unto death. This was the Mahatma's response to the adversary's violence, be it the actual blood-letting of communal mob frenzy or the 'structural' violence of colonial rule. He answered the sin of the adversary by threatening to burden him with more sins, and by scrupulously refusing to commit them himself. Although in his own case he was inspired by the best of motives that of refusing to enlarge the area of human suffering and bloodshed-it has produced among many of his followers, with the exception of a notable few, a moral sanctimoniousness and humbug, which has gone a long way towards discrediting Gandhian amongst the post-independence generations in India.

Many western scholars today, who are aware of the injustice in the world order and its incipient threat to world peace, take interest in the Gandhian model of non-violent conflict as a means of establishing justice and a more egalitarian system.[9] Enthusiasts like Bondurant even refer to satyagraha as a dialectical process, "In every case of satyagraha the conflict is to be understood in dialectical terms. The immediate objective is a restructuring of the opposing elements to achieve a situation which is satisfactory to both the original opposing antagonists but in such a way as to present an entirely new total circumstance".[10]

If we leave aside the dubious distinction of satyagraha as dialectic and follow Gandhi quite literally in his search for 'truth', the inherent illogicality of the above point of view can be seen. In the overall Indian context of satyagraha, the conflict was between two parties, one, the British Government, representative of the humanist society, throughout the major part of the freedom struggle keen on maintaining its profitable position in the Indian subcontinent, and two, the Indian people as led by Mahatma Gandhi, representative of the group society, anxious to restore not only their own sovereignty but their own way of life.[11] There were individuals on the British side, no doubt, who saw the British occupation as an unjust, or futile exercise, and similarly, there were Indians who saw the British presence in India as useful, either in a private or more general capacity. But essentially between the two standpoints, would it make any sense to speak of Indian freedom when finally attained as a 'synthesis' or a situation where there are no winners and no losers? In every instance of confrontation, there was in fact a winner and a loser—sometimes the British and sometime the Indians; the win was effected either outright or by means of a compromise; if there was a 'meeting of minds' it was only on the basis of a realistic assessment of the bargaining position on both sides, and an attempt to hammer out a decision accordingly.

There is no doubt that Gandhi tried to keep the debate at as lofty a level as possible, and to humanize the conflict: it is also true that the British responded with some measure of restraint. But were the two adversaries meeting as equals? In a dialectical or conflict situation, the thesis and antithesis should be roughly equal, but there is no way of seeing the confrontation between India and Britain through satyagraha as one of equality. There is nothing to suggest that before 1947 the British government at all accepted India or her culture as equal and certainly not as superior. They gave into a situation which they could no longer control. There is also plenty of evidence to show that the Indians on their part, did not, with a few exceptions, feel equal and on a par with the British, in spite of Gandhi's efforts to alter that attitude. Indeed the malaise persists till today. In such a situation of superiority and inferiority, where is the synthesis or the 'new truth' or the 'new total circumstance' acceptable to both antagonists? Neither the techniques of violence nor persuasion by themselves can bring about 'truth' indeed when two 'truths' are confronting one another, as they were in India, it was only possible for defeats or frustrations to take place. A great deal depends on one's definition of 'truth' and clearly its usage is too loose in this context. The satyagraha was indeed a means of regulated non-violent conflict and achieved some of the goals of those who waged the conflict. That Gandhi wised to bring about a change of heart in his antagonists does not necessarily imply that it always took place; and if the opponent behaved with respect it cannot be said with certainty whether this was due to conversion by the satyagraha or to his own innate decency.

Compulsion may not have been Gandhi's intention, but in fact this is what his satyagraha did achieve. It pointed out to the opponent not necessarily his untruths, but always his weaknesses. Self-suffering can reduce another to helplessness, disobedient followers can be whipped into line by threats of fasting unto death, executive authority can be challenged by mass civil disobedience. The operational factor was indeed 'suffering' as Gandhi explained: to cause the other suffering and hardship has been one of the classic methods of obtaining compliance (the other being inducement); his own method was to invert the model and attract suffering to himself and his followers in order to obtain compliance-always compliance with justice, he would hasten to append, but compliance all the same. Hence through the use of this inverted suffering there is an undeniable coercive element in satyagraha. It would shed its disguise more readily if it were allowed that in any debated situation there may be more than one truth not a hidden truth, waiting to be revealed to both sides, but two truths at issue, two interpretations of justice. Then the coercive action of the satyagraha becomes clear. He is employing non-violent means (of course better than violent means) to impose his own view of truth and justice upon the particular situation.

This is not to say that each of Gandhi's satyagrahas was based on a doubtful moral issue—far from it, but to point out that the nature of satyagraha is not by itself a guarantor of truth. If one looks at the Indian struggle in its national dimensions, one sees more clearly the operation of two opposing viewpoints. In a reverse almost of the British colonial attitude was Gandhi's uncompromising rejection of western civilization, not only as bad for India but as deficient in itself. He never repudiated a single line of what he wrote in *Hind Swaraj*, which is a clear statement of some of his fundamental convictions. It was not possible for him to enter into a genuine civilisational dialectic with the Englishman, because he did not admit to 'two views on the subject'. Hence any debate that took place would have to be in some neutral region of shared universal morality, but this is a grey area and in practice satyagrahis were warned against expecting total conversion from the other side and advised to seek only for individual conversions. And this brings us closer to the heart of the problem, which is one of defining an area of universal morality apart from civilisational peculiarities.

Gandhi therefore was not so much a fighter for peace, as a peaceful fighter for justice. It is doubtful if the Mahatma can be credited with any constructive activity in the direction of world peace as such, although like all men of goodwill he heartily desired it. No doubt, he felt that perfect peace was an unattainable perfect ideal, and it was more feasible to concentrate on the means, but we know that towards the end of his life he said that ahimsa as means or end was a convertible term. Some have tried to connect the Gandhian struggle-method with peace by suggesting that since conflict is inevitable, a more peaceful society can only be achieved by managing conflict in a non-violent way. And there are always those who believe that only through the regeneration of the individual can peace be achieved, and Gandhi's training of the satyagraha aimed at just that. But this much is clear, that whether in

South Africa or in India, Mahatma Gandhi's concern was with justice and justice only. This is the theme of the Bhagavad Gita also, from which Gandhi drew so much inspiration: without attachment Arjuna must perform his duty of participating in a just war: Gandhi substituted satyagraha for war but justice remained central.

But in the contemporary world, threatened with nevertofore disasters as a consequence of thermonuclear war, the demands of peace are at least on a par with, and for some even override, those of justice, and the game of international relations has become one of uneasy adjustments between the two Perhaps the edge is on the side of peace because no rational mind can contemplate total or near-total extinction, although all would prefer an honourable peace, a peace with justice.

So how is this to be achieved if at all? And to come back to Mahatma Gandhi, is peace at all essentially concerned with either violent or non-violent means? Gandhi's personal philosophy was embedded within the Indian tradition, particularly in the Vedantic view that the many are all aspects or emanations of the one, and that there is an essential unity of life.[12] To mediate between this one and practical life he suggested an inextricable relation between ahimsa and truth, which is God, or the one. Means and ends become inseparable. All the same time, at the level of the everyday, Gandhi is aware that himsa, injury to the living is part of the entire life cycle, unavoidable, so that he is forced to modify his original formulation by advising his followers not to make a 'fetish' out of ahimsa. Many of Gandhi's ethical imperatives are subject to similar qualifications based on realistic or situational considerations. For example, most of the time he inveighs against war as absolutely wrong, yet he would recommend soldiers of a free India to fight for their country. It would be difficult therefore to cull out of his writings and sayings a theory of stable peace.

Notes and References

1. Amiya Chakravarty, 'Gandhi and the Modern World', in G. Ramachandran and T.K. Mahadevan (eds.), Quest for Gandhi, Bombay, Bhartiya Vidya Bhawan, 1970, p. 59.
2. *Ibid.*, p. 60.
3. *Ibid.*
4. Romain Rolland and Gandhi's Correspondence, New Delhi, 1976, pp. 280-81.
5. *Ibid.*, p. 447.

6. Marie Louise Burke, Swami Vivekananda in America: New Discoveries, Culcutta, 1958, pp. 537-66.
7. Jai Narain Sharma, Satyagraha: Gandhi's Approach to Conflict Resolution, New Delhi, 2008, p. 14.
8. *Ibid.*, p. 15.
9. H.J.N. Horsburgh, Non-Violence and Aggression; A Study of Gandhi's Moral equivalent of War, London, 1958.
10. Joan Bondurant, Quest of Violence, Princeton, 1958, p. 195.
11. M.K. Gandhi, *Hind Swaraj,* Ahmedabad, 1975, pp. 94-104.
12. Glynrichards, The Philosophy of Gandhi: A Study of His Basic Ideas, London, 1982.

Freedom, Equality and Peace 5

SURESH SONI

Today, humanity is threatened with total distruction through the development of most sophisticated nuclear weapons. Several crores of rupees are being spent the world over on armaments. If minor portion of this amount could be diverted to peaceful purposes, dramatic and far reaching changes can be achieved in the world. It could be possible to erect an edifice to man which would be a testimony to man's wisdom and his abiding faith in his fellow man. An awareness in developing all over the world that war must be abolished. If we do not abolish war, war will extinguish us. The instinct of self-preservation which is a powerful force, is coming to aid of establishing peace.

When we speak of peace, we do not mean only an absence of overt violence, but also eradication of the roots of violence, such as social and economic exploitation, corruption and concoction, injustice and inequality, 'Making peace involved a reshaping not only of society and in the world order, but also of ourselves.'[1] The choice before us is not between non-violence and violence, but it is between non-violence and non-existence. Hence, the world is fast moving into an era of non-violence. Gandhi declared that 'Non-violence has come to men and will remain, it is the annunciation of peace on earth.'

Food is the basis of life and without it there cannot be any peace and progress in the world. Neither individual morality nor that of the society could take root and thrive on empty stomach. But daily food to all, is attainable for all and that men can realy learn to live together in true human dignity worthy of their divine origin. Gandhi's saying that there is enough in this world for everybody's need and not for everybody's greed has yet to be grasped and made the key to this country's development. Hunger and war can be abolished if only man understood themselves and put themselves in right relationship with man, property and ideas and worked for peace and goodwill on earth.[2]

A best society is one which gives scope and opportunity to every individual for employing all his faculties. Development of all the faculties of man is possible only in a society where man enjoys all the fourfold freedoms—social, economic, political and spiritual. Of all the exploitations, economic exploitation pinches the man most. The greatest of evils and the worst of crimes in our country is grinding poverty. Recent revision of pay scales have to a certain extent helped the employed people. The unemployed and the seasonal wage earner in the rural areas are all still experiencing poverty. The so-called socialists and communists did not bring economic equality today. These people do propaganda in favour of economic equality and to achieve the end they believe in generating hatred. On the contrary, Gandhi's concept of non-violence can bring about economic equality, by converting the people to this desired end by harvessing the forces of love as against hatred. "Working for economic equality means abolishing the eternal conflict between capital and labour. It means the leveling down of the few rich in whose hands is concentrated the bulk of the nation's wealth, on the one hand, and leveling up of the semi-starved, naked millions on the other".[3] So the real meaning of economic equality is "to each according to his needs" as Marx puts it. Gandhi says that "My ideal is equal distribution, but so far as I can see, it is not to be realized. I therefore, work for equitable distribution'.[4] The real implication of equal distribution is that each man shall have the where-withal to supply all his natural needs and no more. As to the requirements of food and clothes, he should have barest minimum possible. This is the spirit of voluntary poverty as practiced and preached by Gandhi. Man should reduce his wants to a minimum, bearing in mind the millions of semi-starved fellow beings. Indeed at the root of this equal distribution, must lie the trusteeship of the wealthy for the superfluous wealth they possessed. The central idea of motive behind trusteeship is a kind of non-violent transformation. It may even be described as non-violent dispossession, most preferably voluntary, but, if necessary, by law. This transfer and non-violent character of this transfer laid the basis for Gandhian conditions of equality.

Gandhi believed that all kinds of work are essential for communal living. He insisted on equal wages for all. He believed "in the division of labour, but at the same time he did not insist on the equality of wages. Only then the division of labour would uplift the nation. There was no other alternative to true civilization".[5] Of course, Gandhi realized that it was too high an ideal to be achieved. Anyhow every nation should set that goal and strive hard to achieve it. Only then economic equilibrium, peace and happiness can be attained.

Unfortunately we find today the so-called youth movements student behavior, strikes and demonstrations do not lay sufficient stress on the need for self-discipline. In the name of grievances, which some people seem to enjoy, they encourage self-indulgence and defiance of established authority. They are symbolic of the spirit of dissent in an aroused nation. Enjoyment is through renunciation, says the Upanisad. We must work for a revolutionary social order in a spirit of dedication.

Gandhi identified himself with humanity, its joys and sorrows, its aspirations and inner seekings. He saw that it was through love alone it would serve it. Love has to be the Law of human beings as that alone can ensure a rational and moral relationship between them. Mutual respect, friendliness, co-operation have to be the forms which love would take. The inner experience of the unity of life and identity of interests cannot and ought not to man anything but the relationship of love between individuals as well as groups and nations.

Gandhi has an undying faith in the innate goodness of man and in the infinite potentialities of love. He said, "AHIMSA means the largest love. It is the supreme law. By it alone, mankind be saved".

Gandhi placed the individual at the centre of his thinking and a deep concern for the inherent dignity of the individual permeates all his theories. He believed that freedom was a basic postulate of morality. He conceived of freedom in terms of 'the freedom of man in all his majesty'.[6]

Gandhi strove hard throughout his life for the attainment of 'PURNA SWARAJ'. Each village should be a self sufficient unit in respect of food, clothes, etc. Every activity should be conducted on the co-operative basis. There would not be untouchability, there would be no unemployment as everyone would work; there would be equality and emanicipation; such a society would be free from the evils of casteism and communalism; people would keep off intoxicating drinks. There would be no poverty nor human degradation. In such a society, people would enjoy the greatest amount of freedom and live on the principle of 'each for all and all for each' and where production would be according to the capacity of the individual and distribution according to his needs. In such a society, people would enjoy freedom and would live peacefully. Gandhi believed in change not for the sake of change but for the establishment of SARVODAYA which is inherently related to his concept of political economy. It is a change in accordance with SVADHARMA, a beneficient change, change for happiness and welfare of all without injuring anyone. It is a change in accordance with the laws of life, aiding man in the future course of evolution towards the more human and humane. Life without love is empty. Knowledge without love is highly dangerous as one sees in the mad race for unclear weapons of the modern age. This integrated philosophy of life namely love informed by knowledge and regulated by virtue runs through his entire philosophy.

It's stressed that the means to achieve a good end must also be good. Gandhi's ideal seems to be only right view of the relation between the end and the means. Good means alone can lead us to everlasting peace. If peace is established we read that armed police, in some places army, marching into an agitating area and peace being established. But that peace is undoubtedly that of 'the grave yard'. But when the non-violent person wins, he wins the heart of the foe.

Peace is an outcome of the application of social and economic non-violence, when they materialize sufficiently. Mankind can avoid military violence only through non-violence. A truly Gandhian technique can fight the evils of corruption, defection, black-marketing or the injustices in economic, individual or social life. It can be an effective technique of change and regeneration where there is no bloodshed, violence or affront to human dignity. Such a change alone will ensure social progress, prosperity and peace.

The modern world is primarily governed by two important aspects of power. One is technological power and the other is the power of human relations. Both are fundamental and are imparting greater influence upon the minds of man. Needless to say that among the virtues that have been cultivated since ages, the power of non-violence is supreme. And when the technological power has started using violence as an instrument of total annihilation of mankind then power of non-violence has started gaining momentum in the mind of civilized man.

For Gandhiji the power of non-violence can be used as a basis for solving every problem. He said, "My daily experience, as of those who are working with me, is that every problem would lend itself to solution if we are determined to make the law of Truth and Non-violence the law of life. For Truth and Non-violence are, to me two faces of the same coin.[7]

The Gandhian non-violence is a social instrument in the struggle for justice and freedom. The faith in non-violence stems from the feeling of solidarity of the whole mankind against conflict and injustice. Today injustice has assumed various forms and power of non-violence is to be directed against it. For Gandhiji non-violence is permanent solution. Therefore, it is dynamic and admits of varied changes in accordance with changing situations. The non-violent approach demands that its adherents must possess positive values of courage, absence of ill-will against the adversary, self control and self abnegation; for non-violence is more powerful than "a thousand suns, Non-violence as a value is higher than life.[8]

Gandhiji regarded that the power of non-violence is a social creed. He believed that non-violence as a weapon of resistance can not gain firm ground unless the attitudes of the people are thoroughly oriented towards non-violence. As D. Dellinger has pointed out in his paper.

"War is but the continuation of the politics of peace by other means and that the social attitude of the society it is defending."[9]

There is strong agreement that the concept of ideal society of Gandhi is based on the power of non-violence, love and the 'good of all' or Sarvodaya. The power of non-violence is the negation of oppression. It promises freedom of the workers from exploitation, of women from the dominance of the male and of untouchables from caste tyranny. Therefore, the principle of non-violence refers to the "Spiritual Power," a sense of moral responsibility, fellow feeling and realistic insight in human psychology. Thus, it fell to the credit of Gandhiji to organize and experiment the power of non-violence in various walks of human life and activity with other dimensions resulting in far-reaching consequences, understanding well the nature of man's destructive, exploitative and impulsive characteristics.

The ongoing matter reveals that power of non-violence is a kind of potent force. It must begin with the mind. The non-violence of the mere body without the co-operation of the mind is weak and has no potency. It is a degrading performance. Because, Ahimsa is a w apon of matchless potency, it is the *summum bonum* of life. It is an attribute of the brave; in fact, it is their all. It does not come within the reach of the coward. It is no wooden or lifeless dogma, but a living and a life giving force. It is the special attribute of the soul. That is why it has been described as the highest Dharma.'[10]

Elaborating the same idea he further mentioned, "My Ahimsa is neither maimed nor weak. It is all powerful. Where there is Ahimsa there is Truth; and Truth is God. He regarded that wherever in the world Truth and Non-violence reign supreme, there is peace and bliss that these exist non-where shows that they are hidden from man for the time being".[11]

Gandhiji believed in Ahimsa as the law of creation and not destruction, "Non-violence is the greatest force at the disposal of mankind. It is mightier than the mightiest weapon of destruction devised by the ingenuity of man because, destruction is not law of human."[12]

Gandhiji further insisted that man must have faith in the power of Ahimsa. He said, "But an ignorance must not be made to serve the cause of disbelief in the power of these forces. Rather is our ignorance a cause of greater faith. Non-violence being the mightiest force in the world and also the most elusive in its working, it demands the greatest exercise of faith. Even as we believe in God in faith, so have we to believe in non-violence in faith."

In this way we can say that power of non-violence is a moral force which makes for social transformation; sooner or later all the people of the world will have to discover a way to live together in peace. If this is to be achieved man must evolve for all human conflicts, a method which rejects revenge, aggression and retaliation. By its very nature non-violence can do more; it can effectively control and guide all power without capturing the machinery of government. That is its unique beauty. As Gandhiji said, "Strength does not come from physical capacity. It comes from an indomitable will.[13]

Gandhiji not only accepted this power of Ahimsa but made it wider to all constructive fields. He said that true Ahimsa would bear a smile even on death-bed brought about by an assailant. It is only with that power that we can be-friend our opponents and win their love.

Lastly, I want to conclude that the sensible human beings of today see in Gandhiji a hope for the integration of mankind, a guide of human relationship and a gospel for spiritual progress. Since the great powers have a moral obligation to mankind they must desist from the ignoble role of fanning hatred and jealousy and pandering to the excessive nationalistic sentiment in contending parties. The developing countries need help to develop their economics, to fight hunger, disease, poverty and ignorance, not arms for their own decimation. The construction of N-bombs and H-bombs are indicators of wiping out entire civilization.

Therefore, presently man is in the horrows of war which will be unparalleled in history. In order to save mankind from these horrors the power of non-violence and its approaches should be adopted everywhere in all disputes whether it may be personal, social and national or international. As St. Paul's first writes that; "Love is patient; Love is kind and envies no one. Love is never boastful. Love will never come to an end."

Notes and References

1. Adam Curle, 'Teaching Peace', Article Published in Everymans, January, 26, 1974.
2. Devadoss, T.S., Sarvodaya and the Problem of Political Sovereignty, University of Madras, 1974, p. 177.
3. Gandhi, M.K., Constructive Programe, N.P.H., Ahmedabad, 1944, p. 18.
4. *Ibid.*
5. Gandhi, M.K., *Harijan,* March 23, 1947.
6. Gnandhi M.K., *Harijan,* November 4, 1939.
7. *Young India,* 1.10.1931, p. 287.
8. Social and Political Thought of Gandhi, J. Bandyopadyaya, 1969, p. 61.
9. *Gandhi Marg,* Vol. IX, October, 1965, p. 228.
10. *Young India,* 6.9.1928, p. 201.
11. *Harijan,* 29.9.1946, p. 332.
12. *Harijan,* 20.7.1935, p. 180.
13. *Young India,* 11.8.1920, p. 3.

Nuclear Explosion and World Peace

Gandhian Solutions

SANJEEV KUMAR SHARMA

6

When *Einstein* was asked what the result would be of a third world-war, he said that after it people would fight with bows and arrows. The scientific-philosopher could not say that the people would not fight. Even before bows and arrows were invented, people fought with stones and before that time they must fought with their teeth, nails and fists. There was fighting and killing all the same. Conflicts are endemic in human societies and are as old as mankind itself. They vary in degree, type, period and societies. It could be either between individuals, groups, organizations, class, section of communities or between nations. Some scholars divided conflicts into interpersonal, intergroup and international. On one hand there are forces of integration and world has contracted into a global village with number of politico-economic and technological and also evolves a vision of borderless world. On the other hand there are equally strong forces fragmenting the nation into pieces.

The 20th century was by far the bloodiest and most destructive century in the history of human race. According to some UN statistics, there was only twenty-eight days in this entire century of genocide and destruction without a war of some kind, in some part of the globe. According to some other estimates, in some period 231 million people were killed or allowed to die by human decisions. Two destructive wars in 1914 and 1939 have set the record of death over 70 million mainly in Europe and Russia. Japan was also partly destroyed by these atom bombs in 1945. War brings destruction and wastage of property. Today over one trillion dollar is being spent on armaments all over the world. *Arundhati Roy* (the author of The God of Small Things) describe the scenario, "Our cities and forests, our fields and villages will burn for days, River will turn to poison. The air will become fire. The wind will spread the flames. When everything there is to burn has burned and the fires die, smoke will rise and shut out of the sun.

Weapon of mass destruction have a peculiar fascination. The great epic-from *Iliad* and *Ramayana* to the *Kalevala* and *Nibelungenlied*—provide thrilling accounts of the might of special weapon, which are not only powerful in themselves, but also greatly empower their possessor.

Whether, or to what extent, powerful weapons empower a nation is not a new question. Indeed, well before the age of nuclear armament began, Rabinder Nath Tagore had expressed a general doubt about the fortifying effect of military strength. If 'in his eagerness of power' Tagore had argued in 1917, a nation 'multiplies his weapons at the cost of his soul, then it is he who is in much greater danger then his enemies'. Tagore was not as uncompromisingly pacifist as Mahatma Gandhi, and his warning against the dangers of alleged strength through more and bigger weapons related to the need for ethically scrutinizing the functions of these weapons and the exact uses to which they are to be put, as well as the practical importance of the reactions and counteraction of others. The 'soul' to which Tagore referred includes, as he explained the need for humanity and understanding in international relations. Tagore was not merely making a moral point, but also one of pragmatic importance, taking into account the responses from others that would be generated by one pursuit of military might. His immediate concern in the quoted statement was with Japan and its move towards extensive nationalism. Tagore was a great admirer of Japan and the Japanese, but felt very disturbed by its shift from economic and social development to aggressive militarism. The heavy sacrifices that were forced on Japan later on, through military defeat and nuclear devastation, Tagore did not live to see (he died in 1941), but they would have only added to Tagore's intense sorrow. But the conundrum that he invoked, about the weakening effects of military power.

J. Robert Oppenheimer, the principal architect of the world's first nuclear explosion, was moved to quote the two-millennia-old Bhagavad Gita (Oppenheimer knew Sanskrit well enough to get his Gita right) as he watched the atmospheric explosion of the first atom bomb in the United States desert near the village of Oscuro on 16 July 1945, the radiance of the thousand suns burst into the sky. Oppenheimer went on to quote further from Bhagavad Gita; I am become death, the destroyer of world. That image of death would show its naked and ruthless face next month in Hiroshima and Nagasaki. Hiroshima and Nagasaki were bombed on August 6 and 9, 1945, respectively. The bomb that was dropped on Hiroshima was of untested design and used 700 gm of enriched uranium as fissile material.

By 1950, it had caused the deaths of over 200,000 of the 3,50,000 people who estimated to have been present in the city on that day. The bomb that was dropped on Nagasaki used plutonium and eventually killed 1,40,000 of the estimated 2,70,000 people present in Nagasaki at that time. "Little boy", the bomb that was dropped on Nagasaki, had a yield of 15 kilotons while "Fat Man", that was dropped on Nagasaki, had a yield of 21 kilotons.

The results were there for all to see-death and devastation on a scale hitherto unknown to humankind. In an atmospheric nuclear weapon explosion, it is the thermal radiation combined with the shock wave that follows that creates the maximum damage. The thermal radiation is intense in a zone around the hypocenter (the point on the ground directly below the atmospheric explosion) whose size is related to the yield of the explosion. The temperature was 600° Celsius at a distance of 1 km from the Hiroshima hypocenter and 1.5 km from the Nagasaki hypocenter. The intensity of the heat was estimated to be seven times that required to burn black paper. Those who were unshielded in this zone suffered from severe third degree burns that lead to death within a weak. The effects of thermal radiation can be attenuated by water and dust particles in the air. Unfortunately, August 6, 1945, was a fine, clear day in Hiroshima. There were instances of fourth and fifth degree burns closer to the hypocenter, with even the tissue below the skin, such as muscle, being destroyed. Closer to ground-zero, the temperature was 15 times that which can cause third degree burns. These thermal intensities are sufficient to flash explodes flesh to steam, leaving the bones bare. The third degree burn zone can extend beyond 10 km for a 1-megaton explosion. The thermal flash can cause a spontaneous combustion of flammable objects and structure of wood, trees and so or their charring, but it does not lead to much self- sustained combustion. What really set off the fires in Hiroshima and Nagasaki was the blast effect of the shock wave that followed. The shock wave begins near ground zero with speeds close to 100 times that of sound. In Nagasaki, this generated winds at over 1,500 km per hour close to ground zero, while 3 km away, it was over 100 km per hour.

The blast wave destroys buildings and other structures, rendering them vulnerable to damage by fire. ·The fire is usually begun by heating appliances, kitchen fires and the like and is aided considerably by the thermal wave that has just passed. Material scattered by the blast help the fire spread. In Hiroshima, the fires began 20 minutes after the explosion, and built up into an intense one, with strong winds blowing into the fire area, with temperatures of up to several hundred degrees. At Nagasaki, it was slow starting, less intense fire (a conflagration), which lasted for five hours. The blast is itself a significant source of damage. A hurricane speed wind is generated with speeds upwards of 180 km per hour. Human beings are killed either by hurtling objects or from impact on hitting walls and other obstacles. Most buildings in the zone collapse. overpressure zone extends beyond 12 km for 1-megaton blasts. A view of what was Hiroshima's main business and industrial centre, shortly after the bomb was dropped. The bomb destroyed 60,000 of the city's buildings in a matter of seconds.

Acute radiation sickness from severe exposure resulted in death within two weeks; those who were exposed to a lesser degree died six to eight weeks later. As for latent effects, the incidence of cancer, particularly leukemia, increased in the period between 1950 and 1953. There was an increase in the number of people who suffered from other kinds of cancer later. Radiation mostly affects those cells in the human body that replicate most rapidly. Children and infants are thus more sensitive to radiation injury than adults. It is, however, fetuses that are the most vulnerable. According to the Radiation Effects Research Foundation at Hiroshima and Nagasaki, unborn children who were exposed to radiation suffer from intelligence quotient impairment, mental retardation and poor physical growth.

There are more than 2200 such weapons, equal to 5000 Hiroshima available even after signing several arms conrol agreements. A technically well equipped nuclear missile can reach any part of the world in less than 30 seconds and destroy completely 140 well developed cities like Tokyo, Washington, Moscow and London. There are also air launcher, submarine launchers and ballistic missiles which are put in alert by nuclear countries such as Israel, North Korea, Argentina and Brazil etc. Those countries are having ambitious plans to produce and deploy such weapons in near future. Therefore, of all the human challenges the threat of nuclear war has been one of the major and dangerous. Because, there are thousands of nuclear weapons have been produced so far and deployed all over the world.

There is no winner or loser in nuclear war. Both the nations at war will be annihilated. Today the magnitude with which the nuclear weapons are made and deployed in and around the world is increasing to 200 to 750 kiloton yields, will cause greater fallout than the megaton range weapons of the 1950's and 1960's. The world has witnessed, as noted various nuclear weapons deployed on the land, sea and in the outer space.

The following is a list of states that have admitted the possession of nuclear weapons, the approximate number of

Country	*Warheads Active/Total*	*Year of First Test*	*CTBT Status*
The five nuclear weapon states under the NPT			
United States	2150/7700	1945 (Trinity)	Signatory
Russia	1740/8500	1949 (RDS –1)	Ratifier
United Kingdom	160/225	1952 (Hurricane)	Ratifier
France	290/300	1960 (Gerboise bleue)	Ratifier
China	n.a./240	1964 (596)	Signatory
Non-NPT nuclear powers			
India	n.a/80-100	1974 (Smiling Buddha)	Non-signatory
Pakistan	n.a/90-110	1998 (Chagai–I)	Non-signatory
North korea	n.a/?10	2006	Non- signatory
Undeclared nuclear powers			
Israel	n.a/80-200	Unknown (possibly 1979)	Signatory

warheads under their control, and the year they tested their first weapon. This list is informally known in global politics as the "Nuclear Club". With the exception of Russia and the United States (which have subjected their nuclear forces to independent verification under various treaties) these figures are estimates, in some cases quite unreliable estimates. Also, these figures represent total warheads possessed, rather than deployed. In particular, under the SORT treaty thousands of Russian and the U.S nuclear warheads are inactive in stockpiles awaiting processing. The fissile material contained in the warheads can then be recycled for use in nuclear reactors.

From a high of 65,000 active weapons in 1985, there are now some 4,100 active nuclear warheads and some 17,000 total nuclear warheads in the world in 2012. Many of the decommissioned weapons were simply stored or partially dismantled, not destroyed.

The leading architect of India's ballistic missile programme and a key figure in the development of nuclear weapons is *Dr. Abdul Kalam*, a scientist of much distinction, recorded his proud reaction as he watched the Indian nuclear explosions in Pokhran, (This was, in fact, the second round of nuclear explosions in the same site, in Pokhran; the first was in 1974) on the edge of the Thar desert in Rajsthan, in May 1998: 'I heard the earth thundering below our feet and rising ahead of us in terror. It was a beautiful sight.' The thousand suns have now come home to the subcontinent to roost. The five nuclear explosions in Pokhran on 11 and 13 May 1998 were quickly followed by six Pakistani blasts in the Chagai hills the following month. 'The whole mountain turned white',was the Pakistani government's charmed response. The subcontinent was by now caught in an overt nuclear confrontation, masquerading as further empowerment of each country.

I remember having read *Vinoba Bhave* saying that he had no objection to the manufacture of atom bomb by the great power, because there manufacture was acting as an effective prevention of war on a wide scale. But *C. Rajagopalachari* announced that nuclear weapons should be banned. Both are right if we understand the reason. The objection of *Vinoba Bhave*'s opinion is that, if several nation possess nuclear weapons, than some mad person or nation may suddenly one day start a nuclear war, which will engulf the whole world *Sh. Rajagopalachari* also is right so long as one nation possessed it. It seems to be reasonable also to desire that the every civilized nation should develop and posssess it; for than no bigger nation will bully and threaten a smaller one. Some of our statesmen assure us that the chief of hope comes from fear.

All the statesman today know that once the nuclear explosion begin, ruin is almost inevitable for every country. Including even one that begins the bombing. We have been thinking about normal men. But what should we say about abnormal men? Unfortunately there is no clear cut distinction as the psychologists tell us between normality and abnormality. Within certain degree, abnormality is not noticed; and below certain still lower degrees, it is not even suspected. Men like *Hitler* are abnormal. If a man is abnormally good, we call him a saint, a bodhisattva, a mahatma. If he is abnormally evil, we call him satanic evil genius. We call neither a lunatic except in a metaphorical case.

I think that the author of our puranas were pessimistic about the ultimate success of ahimsa in this world; otherwise they would not have prophesied that Kalki would be born in the future for destroying the evil doers with the sword in order to establish the humanity that it had a chance to save God from the trouble of incarnating himself as Kalki. However, we need not accept the pessimism of the puranic writer, and we may think about how to establish ahimsa in our world.

Mahatma Gandhi in all his undertaking proved himself to be one of the greatest messengers of peace the world has witnessed and peace became the quintessence of his political philosophy. It is Gandhi's contributions to world peace that the world at large has aptly recognized in him. Gandhi showed the world not only the goal of peace but the supreme method of achieving peace. *George C. Marshall* writes, "In his devotion to peace and tolerance of the brotherhood the mahatma was one of those rare spokesmen for the conscience of all mankind." Peace and tolerance, for Gandhi, were the supreme means for the realization of truth and love which were identical to the ultimate end of man. Gandhi's spiritual, political and economic tenets were permeated by the principal of peace. In the light of peace alone could the human being witness truth.

Gandhi developed his world view against the background of a world of violence. Violence by the foreign rule, economic violence against the poor, political violence against the down trodden and underprivileged, educational violence against the illiterate and background and above all the violence of war and crime. Gandhi's message of peace tool all its sharpness and sensitivity against the background of violence. He says, "What you gain by the violence will be lost greater violence."

Gandhi recognized violence as the root cause of all evils and all evils are thus reducible against the spirit of truth. Hence, from him non violence or ahimsa became the only solution to the problem of life individual, social and national. Hence ahimsa has the great role in the framework of Gandhian thought. Thus, non-violence becomes identified with peace. Peace becomes the true and positive way to the realization of truth. Peace becomes an international goal in the framework of Gandhism. Today peace is the catchword in international relation because the world has come to realized more than ever the vital role of peace in the survival of mankind.

At the time of Gandhi's assassination *Earl Warren* wrote, "The assassination of Gandhi removes from the world by a cowardly act of powerful force for the world peace. Gandhi was essentially a man of peace." The world recognized the Gandhi's contribution to world peace in way's more than the one. Gandhi always set his eyes on world peace as the foundation on which to build a world of truth and love. He says, "Once we accept truth and love as the foundation of our existence, then we have discovered the foundation of unity of humanity. The unity of humanity can be based only on the principal of peace for the development of truth and in hearts of men. Gandhi saw the message of Christ as a unique expression of peace in the world. "I want the help of especially Christians to strengthen my conviction in non violence". Gandhism stands for international peace. It is only through peace that the world can move in the path of truth towards once because thousand of them believe that the message of Christ is that message of World peace and goodwill. Gandhism stands for international peace. It is only through peace that the world can move in the path of truth towards God.

References

Fisher Louis, The life of Mahatma Gandhi (London: Granda), 1982.

Gandhi, M.K., Non-Violence in Peace and War (Ahmedabad: Navjivan Press), 1948.

Jayaprakash, N.D., The Meaning of Hiroshima and Nagasaki (New Delhi; Delhi Science Forum), 1990.

Kenzaburo Oe, Japan, the Ambiguous, and Myself (Tokyo and New York: Kodansha International), 1995.

Moorthy, P., "Value Crises and the way out of World Peace", *Journal of Gandhian Studies*, 2003.

Predrag Cicovacki, "Building a Peaceful World: Mahatma Gandhi and Albert Schweitzer," *Journal of Gandhian Studies*, Vol. 5, Nos. 1 & 2, 2007.

Pruti, R.K., Mahatma Gandhi and World Peace (New Delhi; Common Wealth Publisher), 2009.

Sen Amartya, The Argumentative Indian (Penguin) 2005.

Tagore Rabinderanath, Nationalism (London: Macmillan, 1917; new edn. with an introduction by E.P. Thompson), 1991.

Web site High Energy Weapons Archive at http://www.fas.org/nuk/hew.

Gandhi and Settlement of Disputes 7

Ramesh Kumar

"It is for the thoughtful few," wrote Gandhi in 1924, "to make quarrels impossible by making arbitration popular and obligatory".[1] Gandhi was arguing that communal disputes could be settled by arbitration. "It must be common cause between the two communities that neither party shall take the law into its own hands, but that all points in dispute, whenever and wherever they arise, shall be decided by reference either to private arbitration, or to the law courts if they wish."

According to Gandhi, arbitration is a civilized method of settling disputes. Differences we shall always have but we must learn to settle them all, whether religious or other, whether national or international, by arbitration. In 1939, before the Second World War was declared, Gandhi wrote, "How I wish Herr Hitler would respond to the appeal of the President of the United States and allow his claim to be investigated by arbitrators in whose choice he will have as effective a voice as the disputants."[2] The Indo-British problems, he felt, could be decided by arbitration.[3] On 2 September 1946, the Interim Government was sworn in. The Muslims League did not join the government as they felt that their demands had not been met. Gandhi wrote, "The remedy for injustice if there was any was to reason together or refer the dispute to arbitration in the last resort, if mutual discussion failed."[4]

Junagadh was one of the princely states of India which could legally decide to accede to India or Pakistan when the partition took place in 1947. The ruler of the state was a Muslim; the bulk of the people were Hindus. A provisional government set up in the state decided that the state should accede to India; the ruler decided that it should accede to Pakistan. Indian troops moved into Junagadh. The Pakistan authorities resented this move and contended that the action of the government of India was a clear violation of Pakistan's territory and a breach of international law. Gandhi took the view that arbitration could honourably settle the dispute, If, however, the parties could not agree upon arbitration by Indians, he for one had no objection to any impartial person from any part of the world.[5]

It will thus be seen that Gandhi believed in the utility of arbitration as a method of settling conflicts whether intra-national or international; further, as indicated in the first sentence in this paper, he was for making arbitration obligatory if the parties, for any reason, would or could not go to the courts of law for a decision. Thus the essence of Gandhi's view on the subject is that when a conflict occurs between two parties, it must be referred to a third party (for adjudication by a court or for arbitration) on the correct principle, namely, that no one can be a judge in his own case. One implication of this view, if accepted by society and the government, must be stated: confrontation between employees and employers through strikes and lock-outs will not be permitted.

HOW FAR HAS GANDHI'S IDEA BEEN ACCEPTED IN INDIA?

Let us now examine, briefly to what extent Gandhi's idea on the settlement of conflicts has been accepted.

The Industrial Disputes Act, 1947 provides alternative remedies to deal with an industrial dispute. First, where the appropriate Government is of opinion that an industrial dispute exists or is apprehended, it may, at any time, refer the dispute to a board for promoting settlement thereof, or refer any matter appearing to be connected with the dispute to a court, or to a labour court or a tribunal; the Act also provides for the reference of a dispute to a National Tribunal where the dispute involves any questions of national importance or where the dispute affects industrial establishments situated in more than one State.

Alternatively the employer and the workmen may refer the dispute to an arbitrator or arbitrators agreed upon between them before the dispute has been referred to a Labour Court, a Tribunal or a National Tribunal by government. The arbitration agreement between the parties to the dispute must contain the provision that the parties agree that the majority decision of the arbitrators shall be binding on them. A copy of the Arbitration agreement is to be provided to the Government who will publish the same in the official gazette. Where an industrial dispute has been referred to arbitration and a notification has been issued, the government may prohibit the continuation of any strike or lock-out in connection with such dispute which may be in existence on the date of the reference.

The Essential Services Maintenance Act of 1968 provides that strikes in the essential services such as Posts and Railways may be prohibited by the Government, as a strike therein would prejudicially affect the maintenance of the supplies and services necessary for the life of the community, or would cause grave hardship to the community; in the first instance, the prohibiton of the strike would be for six months.

The Arbitration Act of 1940 provides that parties to a dispute may agree that it may be referred to an arbitrator or arbitrators; there will be an arbitration agreement stipulating the conditions of the agreement. The arbitration agreement will not be invalidated by the death of an arbitrator as provision has been made for the appointment of another arbitrator; similarly, the death of one of the parties will not invalidate the agreement as the legal representatives of the deceased can enforce the agreement. The award of the arbitrator is binding on both the parties.

Even where a suit has been filed in a court, where all the interested parties agree that any matter in difference between them in the suit shall be referred to arbitration, they may, at any time before judgement is pronounced, be referred to arbitration.

Under the scheme of Joint Consultative Machinery inaugurated in 1966-67, compulsory arbitration was accepted in such matters as pay and allowances, bonus and leave applicable to certain categories of central government servants, industrial and non-industrial.

Finally, there is what is known as statutory arbitration. For instance, "the bye-laws framed by the East India Cotton Association under the Bombay Cotton Contracts Act of 1922, making reference to arbitration compulsory as regards the transactions in cotton, coupled with the agreement between the parties to abide by them" have statutory effect having regard to the Bombay Cotton Contracts Act.[6] The Acts where provision for arbitration has been made include the Land Acquision Act of 1894, the Religious Endowment Act of 1863, the Indian Trusts Act of 1882, the Indian Electricity Act of 1910, and the Trade Disputes Act of 1929.[7]

THE NEXT STEP

This brief survey of the extent to which Gandhi's idea of compulsory reference of disputes in domestic conflicts to third-party judgement-by a court or by arbitrators has been accepted boils down to this; in all disputes, voluntary arbitration is permissible; compulsory arbitration exists in regard to some matters affecting pay, allowances, bonus and leave under the Joint Consultative Machinery Scheme applicable to some classes of Central Government employees and workers in Government undertakings; statutory arbitration exists in some fields; in industrial disputes Government has the power to compel reference to courts; and in regard to disputes in essential services, in addition to reference to courts, Government may prohibit strikes.

It will be agreed that in a developing economy like India's, no shortfall in production should be allowed on account of stoppage of work by strikes or lock-outs. In the Railways alone, according to the Railway Minister, an average of 1,32,828 man-days per year was lost during the years 1967-77 excluding the period of 1974 Railway strike; mercifully in 1977-78 the number of man-days lost was only 1858 on account of various measures taken by the Railway management. A strike in the jute industry in January and February 1979 involved 2,20,000 workers and 60 mills in West Bengal, and lasted 49 days. Outside industry, too, we frequently hear of strikes in universities and colleges as well as in medical institutions. Towards the end of February 1979, for instance, strikes were on in the Delhi University Law Centre and University College of Medical Science.

In fields of work outside production like education or maintenance of health, also, strikes are undesirable for obvious reasons.

The only remedy is to create a climate in which every one will accept or be obliged to accept, a third-party judgement in the event of a dispute-judgement by a court or award by arbitration. The Industrial Disputes Act, 1947 and the Essential Services Maintenance Act, 1968 have shown us a method by which the objective could be achieved. Law can provide that a dispute between groups (employees and employers, teachers and students, hospital management and doctors, government and employees' associations) must be settled either by recourse to courts or to arbitration; strikes on any account should not be resorted to. This, in effect, is an extension of the principle-accepted with regard to essential services—to all services on the correct plea that all services may be considered essential to the community. To illustrate the point, Banking is not now in the list of essential services, but the strike of Bank employees (early last year) brought home to everyone Government and people—how essential a services Banking is.

It may be noted that among the trade unions there is some opposition to such a proposal on the ground that the right to strike is a fundamental right. We suggest that reasonable conditions of work including a fair wage may be considered a fundamental right; if this is sought to be secured through a reference to an impartial third party—a court or arbitrators chosen by thc parties when the right is denied, the workers and the society both are gainers. What is fundamental is not the right to strike but the securing of reasonable conditions of work including a fair wage. Securing the right through impartial adjudication or arbitration is a civilized method in contrast to strike which is coercive and disruptive of social harmony. If this correct point of view is put to the workers properly, it may be reasonably hoped that it will receive acceptance from the large majority of them. One suspects that trade unions now oppose the banning of strikes because trade union leaders, the bulk of whom do not belong to the trade and are outsiders, have no interest in the stoppage of strikes.

To ensure successful implementation of such a law, six conditions are essential.

First, the procedure adopted in courts and arbitration tribunals must be streamlined to ensure that unreasonable delay is avoided and cases are disposed of speedily. Confidence in third-party judgement will grow to the extent that decisions are taken speedily. Justice delayed is justice denied, providing an inducement to obtain justice through strikes, gheraoes and such other coercive methods.

Second, there must be a panel of arbitrators maintained and

kept uptodate, both at the national level and the state level. Preferably the panel must be selected in consultation with the Chief Justice of the High Court for State Panels and with the Chief Justice of the Supreme Court for the Central panel.

Third, there must be a well-organized machinery for negotiation and conciliation, always available so that an effort could be made to settle disputes amicably as soon as they arise.

Fourth, workers in industry must be given a sense of belonging to the factory in which they work. In this context, reference may be made to Gandhi's theory of trusteeship. Gandhi wrote on 25 June 1938.

"They (workers) are strong in numbers and yet they feel so dependent, so very much at the mercy of their employers. That is because they do not know their own inherent strength. The thing that they have to realize is that labour is as much capital as metal. The realization of their strength combined with adherence to nonviolence would enable them to cooperate with capital and turn it to people's use. Then they will not regard it as a conflicting interest, they will not regard the mill and the machinery as belonging to the exploiting agents and grinding them down but as their own instruments of production and will, therefore, protect them as well as they would their own property. They will not steal time and turn out less work but will put in the most they can. In fact capital and labour will be mutual trustees, and both will be trustees of consumers. This implies in particular a well-organized scheme for the participation of workers in management, through works Committees or Joint Committees."[8]

Fifth, government must be prepared to abide by the award of the arbitrators where it is a party to the dispute.

And, finally, the political leadership must be able to convince public opinion that the elimination of strikes is in the interest of all. It will take time, but an effort must be made towards that end: To begin with experiments may be more in limited areas, which may later be extended so as to cover all areas and industries. May be as the experiments in India grow and succeed, they will catch the imagination of peoples outside the frontiers of India.

Notes and References

1. A. Appadorai, Documents on Political Thought in Modern India, Vol. I, p. 382.
2. *Ibid.*, p. 382.

3. *Ibid.*, p. 383
4. *Ibid.*, p. 384.
5. *Ibid.*
6. N.D. Basu's Arbitration Act (ed.) S.K. Bose, Calcutta, Eastern Law House Pvt. Ltd., 1969, pp. 809-10.
7. *Ibid.*, p. 812.
8. *Harijan*, 25 June 1938.

Gandhian Alternative for World Peace

8

MONICA SHARMA

The modern society is crisis ridden on all fronts and at the root of all the ills is the crisis of values. Be it the infamous Damini Case of Delhi or hundreds of similar shameful incidents, the numerous political scams that stare at us every other day or the various terrorist activities. The list is endless, hardly a day passes without news indicative of crisis of values. There is erosion of social, moral, cultural, economic and political values at all levels, which has led the spread of selfishness, unlimited greed, corruption, violence and destruction.

The question arises now what can be done to achieve peace and harmony in this scenario. Looking for answers I have zeroed down on Mahatma Gandhi's contribution in this regard that is Peace Education. Gandhiji viewed education as vital in the overall development of individual as well as society. This education has to be given to the students so that they can learn and imbibe the ethics and values of a humanitarian, just, and peaceful society, i.e. Sarvodhya Samaj.

The only solace is that even though we live in a violent world, man fundamentally desires peace. It is acknowledged by all that no positive civilisation, no just social order or stable peace can flow from violence, war and repression. A true social order must be based upon persuasion, conviction and a positive will to co-operate and fellowship among men. These are the only bonds which can hold society together with any permanence and to any real advantage. But because of the difference in world outlook, thinkers, statesmen and politicians differ as to the effective way of establishing just and lasting peace.

The Gandhian thought of peace is worldwide acknowledged. The name of Gandhi is synonymous with peace & non-violence. That is why United Nation announced World Peace Day on 2nd October, the birth date of Mahatma Gandhi.

Before elaborating on the Gandhian notion of peace education, we need to locate what peace education broadly means. Peace education can be understood as education for facilitating peace. According to Peace Education Working Group at UNICEF, peace education "refers to the process of promoting the knowledge, skills, attitudes and values to prevent conflict and violence."

It is the transmission of knowledge about the requirements of, the obstacles to and the possibilities for achieving and maintaining peace. In 1945, the United Nations was established to "save succeeding generations from the scourge of war and to establish conditions under which justice and respect for the obligations arising from treaties and other sources of international law could be maintained. Peace education has developed as a means to achieve these goals. According to the preamble of the UN Charter Peace education is "directed to the full development of the human personality and to the strengthening of respect for human rights and fundamental freedoms".

The field of peace education, originating in the post-World War II period seeks to address direct, structural and cultural forms of violence through the transformation of educational content and structure. Though the field originally focused on the elimination of direct violence, emphasising nuclear disarmament and countering militarism, one of the core goals of peace education has also become the elimination of cultural and structural violence, which are rooted in social inequalities that limit access to resources and opportunities for individuals and groups and may be embedded in longstanding cultural practices, attitudes or Patterns

Peace education aims to reduce violence, support the transformation of conflicts and advance the Peace capabilities of individuals, groups, societies and institutions. It builds on the capacities of the people to learn, develop skills, values and knowledge and thus help to establish a global and sustainable culture of peace.

There is no uniform concept of peace education and the international discourse on this topic is still in its infancy.

The importance of peace education for peaceful co-existence is emphasised in the UNESCO Preamble which states that "since wars begin in the minds of men, it is in the minds of men that the defences of peace must be constructed." This statement and its critical assessment have shaped the conceptual development of peace education.

Peace education pursues the following goals :

- To end war.
- To reduce violence in family, society and politics.
- To develop visions of peace and solidarity among the people of the world.

Originally aimed at eliminating the possibility of global extinction through nuclear war, peace education currently addresses the broader objective of building and sustaining a culture of peace. In this global effort, progressive educators world-wide are teaching the values, standards and principles articulated in fundamental UN instruments such as the UN Charter, Human Rights documents, the Convention on the Elimination of All forms of Discrimination Against Women (CEDAW), and many others. Many teachers are already practising peace education without calling it by name. Historically, in various parts of the world, peace education has been referred to as Education for Conflict Resolution, International Understanding, and Human Rights, Global Education, Education for Liberation and Empowerment, Social Justice Education, Environmental Education, Life Skills Education, etc. These various labels illuminate the depth and diversity of the field. Using the term peace education helps co-ordinate such global initiatives and unite educators in the common practice of educating for a culture of peace.

Peace is an essential component of quality basic education. It is the process of promoting the knowledge, skills, attitudes and values needed to bring about behaviour changes that will enable children, youth, and adults to prevent conflict and violence both overt and structural, to resolve conflict peacefully and to create the conditions conducive to peace, whether at an intrapersonal, interpersonal, national or international level. The 1990 World Peace Declaration on Education for All says that...every person-child, youth and adult shall be able to benefit from educational opportunities designed to meet their basic learning needs. these needs comprise both essential learning tools such as literacy, oral expression, numeracy and problem-solving and the basic learning content such as knowledge, skills, values and attitudes required by human beings to be able to survive, to develop their full capabilities, to live and work in dignity.

This is quite similar to the Gandhian approach relating to value and Buniyadi Shiksha which according to him was important for construction of a sustainable culture of peace. *Buniyadi Shiksha* or Basic Education also known as '*Nai Talim*' was the base of educational practice as propounded by Gandhi in 1937 at Wardha which subsequently was known as Wardha Scheme or Basic National Education.

Though the word Buniyadi, which Mahatma Gandhi used in the twentieth century, meant the knowledge or education that could help people in the promotion of handicrafts or to establish cottage industries, it is the basis of the technical education of the twenty-first century. As the ultimate purpose behind his thoughts and attempt was to make young men and women self-reliant in the economic field, even in the modern perspective, his idea of Buniyadi or basic education is equally relevant and quite similar to the concept of today's job-oriented or technical education the aim of both is to it make a man self-dependent and prosperous. And such a person can, definitely, contribute towards peace and prosperity of society and the nation.

For Gandhi, peace can be located in "his revolutionary mode of action which he called *satyagraha*, and his challenging goal of *sarvodaya*, meaning the welfare and good of all. Peace to Gandhi is primarily located in his idea of *Ahimsa* i.e. non-violence, however, his ideas of trusteeship and passive resistance both form the base for a peaceful and just society.

Gandhi made great contribution to the cause of world peace and his views therefore demand close scrutiny. He has been rightly described as an apostle of peace. He strove and died for peace he advocated peace—but not at any price. The Peace he advocated is integrally related to justice. He did not share the diplomatic view of peace. Peace for him connoted a positive state of affairs the pre-condition being freedom from exploitation. What he advocated was non-violent and just peace which alone in his opinion could ensure lasting peace.

Mahatma Gandhi looked upon the problem of War as the most important problem facing the contemporary world. He believed that unless we are able to devise a method of collective action which would be more efficient than war in the resolution of conflicts, humanity would be involved in a race for armament which might prove disastrous and suicidal. He explained his concept of non-violent peace while talking to the Christian missionaries in 1938, Peace will never come until the Great Powers courageously decide to disarm themselves. I have a faith that after half a century's experience of unbroken practice of non-violence that mankind can only be saved through non-violence.

The idea of *sarvadharmasamabhava* i.e. equality of religions as espoused by Gandhi is an effective tool to counter the increasing tensions among different religious groups. According to Gandhi, "a curriculum of religious instruction should include a study of the tenets of faiths other than one's own. For this purpose, the students should be trained to cultivate the habit of understanding and appreciating the doctrines of various great religions of the world in a spirit of reverence and broad-minded tolerance. This, if properly done, would help to give them a spiritual assurance and a better appreciation of their own religion. This study of other religions besides one's own will give one a grasp of the rock-bottom unity of all religions, and afford a glimpse also of that universal and absolute Truth which lies beyond the 'dust of creeds and faiths.'

Thus we see Gandhian concept is, ever relevant for achieving the goal i.e., peace—or for construction of a real and sustainable culture of peace, especially under the democratic system of government. In this context, its relevance and importance of its role can never be underrated. It should be applied in wider perspective. The need of the day is to take up, adopt and understand Gandhian approach according to time and space and to put it into practice in the process of education, the world over.

References

Bose, Anima, A Gandhian Perspective on Peace in the *Journal of Peace Research*, XVIII (2), Norway International Peace Research Institute, 159-64.

Gupta, A.K. Das, Gandhi on Social conflict, *Economic and Political Weekly.* [Volume I-III, No. 49]. Mumbai, 1876-78.

Harris, Ian and Marry, M. Lee Morris, 2003. On Peace Education [Second Edition]. USA: North Carolina: McFarland.

Kumar, Manju and Raghuvansh, Sujata. Locating Education for peace in Gandhian Thought. Mumbai: GSM. http://www.mkgandhi.org/articles/peace_education.htm.

Page, James, 2008. Peace Education: Exploring Ethical and Philosophical Foundations, U.S.A: Information Age Publishing.

Ravi, S. Samuel. 2011. A Comprehensive Study of Education, New Delhi: Prentice-Hall of India Pvt. Ltd.

Singh, M.K. and Kumar, A., 2007. Reading Gandhi, New Delhi: K.K. Publications.

Security Without Violence

A Gandhian View

9

SHIVALI KAPOOR

INTRODUCTION

Human security is a new concept. Human security is a people-centered concept. This concept first came into existence by the global 1994 Human Development Report of the United Nation's Development Programme. This report shifted the concept of security from the protection of state and its borders by military means to the protection of individuals from a wider range of threats to their well-being and security. Traditionally the concept of human security was limited to the protection of states and its boundaries by preparing armed forces but now the concept of human security has changed and it is having wider range of measures and policies from the local and the community level to the national and international arena.

With the end of the cold war and demise of the Soviet Union by 1991, the United Nations strategy for dealing with conflicts shifted from containment to prevention. In 1992, the United Nation's Secretary General issued "An agenda for Peace, Peace-making and Peace- keeping—Early optimism for a more peaceful world". However,this optimism was dashed by a rising number of conflicts in developing countries. These were overwhelmingly internal conflicts, though sometimes national groups received external support. Most of these conflicts were outside the interstate model espoused by the realist.

The cause of these conflicts were seen to be linked to non state and non-traditional factors such as internal socio-political conditions, rapidly deteriorating economic conditions, environmental threats, identity politics and powerful organized crime rings.

In an attempt to address these transformations, the United Nations system once more engaged with alternative views of security, articulating the concept in terms of a reframed emphasis on the empowerment of individuals by addressing system policies and practices that contributed to insecurity. Despite having embodied the concept of 'collective security' since its inception and having witnessed the transformation of the concept beyond its original parameters during the cold war competition of superpower interest, the United Nations increasingly championed alternative approaches to development and security. Infact, this alternative focus on 'people' as the referent object of security is evident in the United Nations initiatives on human rights almost from the beginning.

Human security first had an official standpoint in world politics with the unanimous adoption of the "Universal Declaration on Human Rights, 1948" and the subsequently in the "International Covenant on Civil and Political Rights (1966)", "The International Covenant on Economic, Social and Cultural Rights (1966)", "The Covenant on the Elimination of All Forms of Discrimination Against Women (1979)" and "The Covenant on the Rights of the Child (1989)" can all be seen as elements of alternative perception of security. Each of these conventions and covenants focused on various vulnerabilities and threats experienced by individuals.

CONCEPT OF HUMAN SECURITY

Human security represent an effort to re-conceptualize security in a fundamental manner. It is primarily an analytical tool that focuses on ensuring security for the individual. Thus, exploring options aimed at mitigating threats to the insecurity of individuals thus becomes a central concern in policy recommendations and actions. Individual safety and freedom are immutable values at least in any liberal political philosophy. Sensitivity towards security for the individual existed from the middle of 17th century upto the French Revolution. However, after French Revolution organized violence between states escalated that consequently paved way for all the pervasive concept of security. Human security concern with personal safety and freedom does not emerge due to the deterrence caused by the consequences that may flow from their non protection but rather because these are morally worthy values that must be upheld for their own sake. Human security requires an audit of the threats to safety and freedom. This audit will define the paradigm of human security.

The ideas circumscribing the concept of human security are subject to change and expansion under the ever expanding notion of welfare state. So, as to develop the record of safety and freedom of the individual all over the world. The human security with the end of the cold war calls for rethinking in security matters grew rapidly.

In 1991 the Stockholm initiative on Global security and Governance issued a call for "Common Responsibilities in 1990" which referred to challenges to security other than political rivalry and armaments and to "a wider concept of security which deals also with the threat that stems from failure in development, environmental degradation, excessive population growth and movements and lack of progress towards democracy".

In line with the expanded definition of human security, the causes of human security are subsequently broadened to include threats to socio-economic and political conditions, food, health, and environmental community and personal safety.

Human security is therefore people centred, multidimensional, interconnected and universal. In principle, it reflects the aggregate gains as a result of the mitigation of each and every factor that contributes to insecurity United Nation's Development Programme's 1994 definition.

Dr. Mahbub-ul-Haq first drew global attention to the concept of Human Security in the United Nations Development Programme's Human Development Report.

The United Nations Development Programme's Human Development Report while defining human Security argues that the scope of global security should be expanded to include threats in seven areas.

Economic security—Economic security required an assured basic income for individual, usually from productive and remunerative work or, as a last resort, from a publicly financed safety net.

Food security—Food security requires that all people at all times have both physical and economic access to basic food.

According to the United Nations, the overall availability of food is not a problem, rather the problem often is the poor distribution of food and lack of purchasing power. In the past, food security problems have been dealt with at both national and global levels.

However, their impacts are limited. According to United Nations, the key is to tackle the problems relating to access to asssets, work and assured income (related to economic security.

Health security—Health security aims to gurantee a minimum protection from diseases and unhealthy lifestyles. In developing countries, the major causes of death traditionally were infectious and parasitic diseases, whereas in industralised countries, the major killers were diseases of the circulatory system.

Today, lifestyles related chronic diseases are leading killers worldwide, with 80% of death from chronic diseases occurring in low and middle-income countries.

According to the United Nations in both developing and industrial countries, threats to health security are usually greater for poor people in rural areas, particularly children. This is due to malnutrition and insufficient access to health services, clean water and other basic necessities.

Environmental security—Environmental security aims to protect people from the man-made threats in nature, and deterioration of the natural environment. In developing countries lack of access to clean water resources is one of the greatest environmental threats. In industrial countries one of the major threat is air pollution. Global warming caused by the emission of greenhouse gases, is another environmental security issue.

Personal security—Personal security aims to protect people from physical violence, whether from the state or external states, from violent individuals and sub-state actors, from domestic abuse, or from predatory adults. For many people the greatest source of anxiety is crime, particularly violent crime.

Community security—Community security aims to protect people from the loss of traditional relationships and values and from sectarian and ethnic violence.

Political security—Political security is concerned with whether people live in society that respects their basic human rights. Human rights violation are most frequent during periods of political unrest. Along with repressing individuals and groups, governments may try to exercise control over ideas and information.

Since then human security has been receiving more attention from the key global development institutions, such as World Bank.

Shahrabanou Tadjbakhsh among others, traces the evolution of human security in international organizations, concluding that the concept has been manipulated and transformed considerably since 1994 to fit organizational interest.

GANDHI'S CONCEPT OF HUMAN SECURITY

Although the concept of human security has evolved in the last quarter of twentieth century, with the coming up of Human Life Index and Human Security Index, irrespective of this fact, while studying Gandhi's social and political philosophy it is not difficult to see several elements and essentials of the human security concept already been given a significant place in the Gandhian framework of truth, non- violence and dignity of the individual.

According to Gandhi security is a holistic phenomenon. Gandhi is in favour of a non-violent and more civilized life style. According to Gandhi, highest form of security is possible in a civilized and gentle world where armed battalions do not coerce. Until there is widespread voluntary effort towards conflict transformation by individuals and states alike, the cities of the world will not have rest from armed conflicts, wars and mass murders.

Gandhi says weapons cannot provide security to individuals. It is the morale and faith in God and truth that leads to real sense of security. Modern weapons and technology leads to widening of net of insecurity among peoples and modern armies. The Gandhian conception of security can provide a great sense of strength and conviction to modern global citizens. However for this, a process of transformation has to begin for helping evolve a general confidence in the ways of Gandhian non-violence. His vision is characterized with holistic perception of truth, foresightedness and scientific analysis. Gandhi envisioned human security as a natural corollary of peace and development and not something which is inextricably linked with military might.

Gandhi asserts under Swaraj (self-rule) of my dream there is no necessity of arms at all.... but also in my Swaraj of today there is room for soldiers.... I have not the capacity for preaching universal non-violence to the country. He laments the existing peculiar sense of security replete with threats of human extinction where in modern security is possible through mutual assured destruction.

Mahatma Gandhi is known as a proponent of non-violence and peace in the world. He has widely written on war, peace and security *vis-a-vis* individuals states and broader global perspectives. Gandhi however is a "practical idealist." Gandhi vision is alive with holistic perception of truth and scientific analysis.

Gandhi sees inherent linkages between knowledge, virtue or wisdom on the one hand and security of a civil society comprising understandably connected individuals, groups, administrative units, polis of different magnitudes, provinces sovereign states, international and global organizations on the other hand. This is very clear line of thinking and continued relationship amongst these aspects of security from the level of an individual to an international establishment and global order.

As such, Gandhi's view of security for both an individual and a state can have meaning only through certain inter-related measures taken by the world community of nations over a period of time. These measures are :

- Global conventional and nuclear disarmament.
- Prevention of environment and ecology.
- Resolving the population, poverty, and unemployment menace.
- Thinking more about peace than about war and weapons.

Peace and development through security are the essence of modern conception of security. Instead for Gandhi, security is possible through peace and development only. The major difference in these two views is primarily that of emphasis.

The Gandhian perspective considers security as a natural corollary of development and peace. It is not weapons and machines but pulsating human beings who are of real significance.

Gandhi is critical of the so-called civilized world as he remarks—" this civilization is one where one has to be patient and it will be self- destroyed. "Gandhi's concept of human security is holistic one where in the emphasis non-violence as a way of life and asserts that it is a morale and faith in God that leads to a real sense of security.

Real holistic security for Gandhi is possible only through Panchyama of Patanjali, i.e non-violence (ahimsa), non-stealing (astaeya), truth (satya), non-possession (aparigraha) and chastity (bramcharaya). Gandhi envisions a non-violent society as the ultimate ideal for establishing a vibrantly creative global and political ethical world as he believes that cultivation of non-violence by individual and the establishment of a non exploitative economy at different levels will be eventually lead to the emergence of what he calls non violent nationalism.

The concept of human security on the global political scene has been adopted by various organizations to conform to different political agendas. International organizations and commissions have used their moral authority to encourage states to improve their citizens lives. They have sought to revive collective and individual conscience. Yet as Grayson remarks — trying to find a workable definition for human security is a question of politics and search for power, in-fact endorsement of well defined acceptance of human security by Canada (freedom from fear) and Japan (freedom from want) was determined by policy utility.

While Canadian conception of human security as freedom from fear, i.e fear of physical, psychological, sexual harassment, fear of health, job, violence, death, etc. and focus on human right as justification for interventionist foreign policy. Japan support for human security as freedom from want i.e want of gainful and employment opportunities which concentrates on human development. To understand United Nation's Development Report approach to human security we need to understand an answer four key questions :

- Security for whom.
- Security for which values.
- Security from what threats.
- Security by what means.

If we compare United Nation's Development Programme School to Canadian School of Human Security we can highlight the following differences.

Security for whom according to United Nation's Development Programme is about the 'individual' whereas in Canadian it is about individual as well as 'state'.

Security of what values—according to both United Nation's Development Programme School and Canadian School is about personal safety.

Security from what threats—according to United Nation's Development Programme School there is greater emphasize on indirect violence and whereas for Canadian School it emphasize on direct violence.

Security by what means according to United Nation's Development Programme it is by promoting human development and where as for Canadian school it is by promoting political development.

Human security can be viewed as the protection of individuals from risks to their physical or psychological safety, dignity and well-being. An environment that can be said to provide its members with human security is one which afford individuals the possibility to lead stable, self-determined lives.

Human security are basic rights grounded in the dignity of each human being whether their foundational bases comes from human nature, human reason or natural law.

State should take steps to the maximum of its available resources, with a view to achieving progressively the full realization of economic rights. The relationship between human rights and human security is symbiotic because human rights leads to human security and it empowers people to seek solution in a right barred approach.

Humanitarian intervention one of the ways in which states and international organizations have tried to impose human security in certain areas of the world. The concept of human security has significantly changed the notion of international intervention. Sovereignty is now considered a responsibility. If human security is a collective responsibility than this responsibility lies in the coordinated action of actors at all levels who must act in the framework of law.

The ideal type of human security approach envisaged the state to be a part of a dynamic and seamless policy network with non-state actors including NGO's and civil society, international and regional organizations as well as individuals and their communities. In the human security conception the primary referent of security is the individual. Human security does not ignore state security, but it treats it as no more than co-equal to individual security.

The key argument is that ultimately state security is for individual security. Only the security of the individual can be the rightful and meaningful objective of security. Two values are paramount in the human security conception : the bodily safety of the individual; and his personal freedom.

CONCLUSION

Human security is a universal concern. It is relevant to people everywhere, in rich nations and poor. The components of human security are interdependent. Human security is people-centred. It is concerned with how people live and breathe in society, how freely they exercise their many choices, how much access they have to market and social opportunities and whether they live in conflict or in peace.

Gandhi conceives a peaceful world order as :

1. It should be non violent.
2. It must be non-exploitative and cooperative.
3. It has to be based on the reform regeneration and education of the individual.
4. It must work its way up to the global or international level through reform or non-violent reorganization.

Gandhi has spoken and written profusely on non-violence, security, peace, war, conflict, world order, and world federation of nations, etc. Comparatively speaking the Gandhian conception of Security was far ahead of its times as the formalization of the term Human Security occured in 1990s.

Human security in its broadest sense embraces for more than the absence of violent conflict which was ever-emphasized by Gandhi. It encompasses human rights, good governance, access to education and health care and ensuring that each individual has opportunities and choices to fulfil his or her own potential. Every step in this direction is also a step towards reducing poverty, achieving economic growth and preventing conflict. Freedom from want, freedom from fear and the freedom of future generations to inherit a healthy natural environment-these are the interrelated building blocks of human and therefore national security.

References

Charter of the United Nations [www.un.org/aboutun/charter/preamble.htm].

Walker, R.B.J., 1997. 'The Subject of Security'. Critical Security Studies.

Boutros-Ghali, B., An Agenda for peace, peace making and peace-keeping. A report of the Secretary-General Pursuant to the statement adopted by the Summit Meeting of the Security Council on 31 January: United Nations, DPI/1247, New York, 1992.

Buzan, B.O. Waever and J.de Wilde., Security: (A New Framework for Analysis. London: Lynne Reinner Publisher), 1998, pp. 22-23.

Kaldor, M., New and Old Wars: Organised Violence in a Global Era. (Polity Press/Stanford University Press), 2001, p. 9.

Mahbub-ul-Haq, Reflections on Human Development (Oxford: Oxford University Press), 1995.

Sen, A., Development as Freedom (Oxford: Oxford University Press), 1999.

Tadjbakhsh, S., "Human Security In International Organisations: Blessing or Scourge?", *The Human Security Journal*, Volume 4, Summer 2007.

World Health Organisation, "Chronic Diseases" http://www.who.int/topics/chronic_diseases/en/

Thomas, N. and Tow, W.T., The Utility of Human Security: Sovereignty and Humanitarian Intervention, *op. cit.*

Mahatma Gandhi ,Concept of Global Security and Peace, Anurag Gangal. http://www.gandhitopia.org/profile/Anurag Gangal.

Peace and Human Security

An Analysis in Different Perspectives

10

SURESH KUMAR JAGLAN

"There is no way to peace, peace is the way".

—Mahatma Gandhi

Peace should not be understood in military terms, like absence of armed conflicts. Peace should be understood in a human way in a brood social, political and economic way. Peace should mean social justice between nations and within nations. It should mean establishment of human right for all people.[1]

In the new context, the concept of "Peace" would be the existence of a political and economic environment where each human being is truly free from the control of any powerful person or any powerful nation, free from poverty, hunger and indignities and free to explore the limits of one's potential.

The concept of peace in our modern Civilization is the façade of war, dominated by the calculations of realpolitik. This English Word originates from, the French concept which denotes 'agreement'—agreeing to stop a conflict or war.[2] According to the Universal Dictionary of the English Language, the first notion of 'peace' is cessation of freedom from strife, welfare, and the second notion of it is 'treaty of peace between hostile nations.' According to the third notion, it is understood as, freedom from strife, controversy or agitation or freedom from civil disorder and disturbances. These notions tranquility, concord, mental calm, serenity of mind crystallized into common place word, Universally understood and emphasized by teachers and preachers alike, also enshrined in scriptures of all religions and beliefs.[3]

Peace interaction must be based on mutual self-respect and a positive need to internalize and appreciate any form of reciprocation. They are not to be stratified response in terms of a position. All involved are facilitators and also learners. The learning experience must be that of equalitarian sharing. In order to fully comprehend how we educate ourselves in dialogue, let us be aware of the following realities. In our interaction with each other, we wish to be part of the following processes. We wish to be part of the following processes. We wish to become acquainted with, gain insight to appreciate, and attempt to experience a landscape that is both interior to us. We do not aim at being enlightened in the academic sense but wish to have within our grasp a self awareness of things that are meaningful, accurate, precise, and helpful to self-propelled growth towards peace.

Hindu, Jain and Buddhist traditions treat peace as peace of mind, peace of the inner self, interpersonal peace and non-violence, the moral injunction of not committing violence against nature and also against micro-organism.[4]

Peace has the potential to mean many things. The definitions of Peace can vary with religious, social, cultural or the study of things. However, two dominant interpretations of peace exist as negative peace and positive peace.

Negative peace is defined as "State requiring a set of social structures that provide security and protection for the acts of direct physical violence committed by individuals, groups or nations. This type of "violence includes physical violence where the actor is visible and action is direct e.g., if a group of persons attacks another group of persons. This is a case of direct violence." Direct violence can be divided into verbal and physical violence harming the body mind and spirit. This leaves behind traumas that may carry violence over time. In highly dynamic society, personal or direct violence and child violence.

The positive concept of "peace would lead us to consider not only absence of direct violence and structural violence, but also presence of a non-violent type of egalitarian, non-exploitative and non-suppressive cooperation between units-nations as well as individuals".

The struggles for peace and action to promote human rights are recognized as being inseparable. The UN systems do not define peace only as the absence of war and violence but also as the presence of justice.[5]

Gandhi equated peace with non-violence and satyagraha and its determinant is the achievement of truth. His non-violence ruled out all exceptions in the applications of Ahimsa. His concept of non-violence is very broad. His non-violence doesn't include only non-killing but also cultivation of love, compassion and altruism to all. We should not trust anybody in actions, words and deeds. He tries to apply non-violence in every walk of life—domestic, institution, economic and political. "peace is outcome of the application of non-violence at intra-personal, social economic, political, cultural and religious levels", he said.[6]

PEACE IN THE POLITICAL PERSPECTIVE

Democracy is a great idea, but it has been badly understood in relation to inter-state affairs. If a democracy works well within a country, it will in principal, produce a relatively content population that on the average and over time, gets much of its wishes fulfilled, within the limits of the feasible. Again in principle, this lead to a peace surplus inside the country with democracy functioning as a non-violent arbiter between parts of the population vying with each other for power and privilege But there is no guarantee that this intra-state peace surplus will translate into peaceful activity in the inter-state system.

Democracy has to be global in the inter-state system in the world system. But that system is today conservative-fended not liberal-democratic.

PEACE IN THE MILITARY PERSPECTIVE

The argument made here is not to abolish the military but to give it new tasks. That institution had very bad habits in the past, such as attacking other countries and nations, and other classes usually at the behest of the ruling elites, killing and devastating through external and internal wars.

Let us give the military new tasks, substituting defensive defense with defensive means for aggressive external warfare. Pure defense provokes nobody and causes no fear yet makes it clear that attacks will be strongly resisted.

Peace-keeping forces can be used to prevent aggressiveness even in places where there has been no open display of violence.

The struggle against the tendency of states to seek recourse to military power goes by way of alternatives that are more compelling and the struggle against hegemonic tendencies in the world society of societies goes by way of democratization of that society, creating alliances of non-hegemonic countries within or across their spheres of interest, and through decision-making of our country, one vote variety.

PEACE IN THE ECONOMIC PERSPECTIVE

The problem here is not only economic practice but also economic theory with its carefully nursed neglect of the side-effect of economic activity the externalities. Some of them are positive, like the challenge derived from taking on complex problems for which there are no immediate, routine solutions. And some of them are negative, like ecological degradation, not to mention human degradation. They are not reflected in economic theory, or at most as side and after-thoughts, economists focus on quantities and prices of products, goods and services offered in the market place without reflecting whether they might also be bad and disservices. Such variables are referred to as internalities internal to the paradigm.

PEACE IN THE CULTURAL PERSPECTIVE

Why do people kill? partly because they are brought up that way—not directly to kill, but to see killing as legitimate under some conditions, that brings us to culture, that great legitimizer of violence, but also of peace. Where do we find the key carriers of violence? The easy answer would be 'religion and ideology' since people are known to kill in the name of either. However, not ill religions or ideologies are violent, some are even outspoken in their advocacy of non-violence or to use the formulation preferred here, religions and ideologies can come in hard and soft varieties the harder varieties tending to focus on some abstract, transcending goal and the softer ones on empathy even compassion.

HUMAN SECURITY

The moment human being came into this world, his search for security begins. In the history of mankind his sense of survival has been the most powerful motivating force. Security has been one of the several basic drives for people to come together in communities. Men have shown their faith in the prince or the king for their security as a collective unit. Security has always been an important element of the responsibilities of leadership and authority.

With the passage of time the meaning and scope of security has become much broader. The threshold of the new millennium is also the cusp of a new era in world affairs. The business and politics of the world has changed almost beyond recognition over the course of the last one hundred years. There are many actors in politics and their patterns of interaction are far more complex. The focus of power and influence is shifting. The demands and expectations made by governments and the international organizations of the world are also changing. Individuals have found diverse ways to secure their security.[7]

The term 'security' presents the feeling of peace and harmony at psychological level a feeling of being well guarded for several uncertainties. Although security is a contested concept yet there is a consensus that security implies 'freedom from threats to core values'.[8]

The idea of human security developed in the context of the UN in the mid-1990s. In the beginning this concept largely focused on the problem of advancing opportunities for human development. But the focus soon shifted to an understanding of security based on Universal human rights. The classic definition of human security is related to two aspects of freedom, namely "Freedom from want" and "freedom from fear". In contrast to the narrow traditional as well as the expanded concept of security, which emphasize state actions, the concept of human security sees the individual as the key actor. It highlights the more neglected aspects of human developments and human rights in foreign and security policy debates, giving these issues new visibility.[9]

Human security is an emerging paradigm for understanding global vulnerabilities whose proponents challenge the traditional notion of national security by arguing that the proper referent for security should the individual rather than the state.

Small arms and landmines are grim examples of threats to human security. We know that once a conflict has ended, these weapons remain- stockpiled, buried, hidden or in circulations. In addition to posing the very real threat of physical harm, they have enduring consequences in vulnerable and fragile societies, inhibiting reconstruction, development and an eventual return to normalcy. Their victims are predominantly civilians and too often they are children.[10]

During the cold war, the prevailing security concepts were based on notions of absolute security implying that one side's security was to be achieved at the expense of the respective other's security. Deterrence and arms racing characterized mainstream security policies throughout this period and the arms race became so all-pervasive that no nation was able to stand aloof from it, yet without net gains in security.

Only belatedly did nations arrive at an understanding of the 'Security dilemma' phenomenon, on the basis of which security experts proposed alternatives to absolute security that would contribute to a world of peaceful coexistence including concepts of mutual security, common security and cooperative security.[11]

In the modern age, Security cannot be obtained Unilaterally and the security of one nation cannot be bought at the expense of others. The danger of nuclear war alone assures the validity of this proposition. Mutual security policies thus aim at improving the security of both Sides under conditions of some mutual insecurity-a precept that is valid not only for two nations but also for two alliances or two militant organizations threatening each other. Mutual confidence-building endeavour requires compromising poser.[12]

Nations seeking to enhance their own Security be means of increased threats against others inevitably find themselves facing a security dilemma, as they achieve a loss of security as a paradoxical result of their quest for security. The more defense measures one nation adopts in order to increase its sense of security, the more insecure the other feels. As a consequence thereof, the latter nations responds with further defence measures that render the former nation feel less secure, etc. The national security of both sides is thus reduced and both intensify efforts to at least equal security level.[13]

Common security advocates the view that international peace must rest on a commitment by each nation to joint survival rather than on threats of mutual destruction. The security of the world becomes increasingly interdependent as interdependence grows among nations in the political, diplomatic and economic domains. Hence, one nation's pursuit of its national security may endanger global security in a world devoid of authority that might control the pursuit of security by individual nations by adopting a global persective.[14]

The Concept of cooperative security implies that nations seek to achieve national security by pursuing only such objectives as are compatible with the security of other nations and that they seek collaborative rather than confrontational military relations. Cooperative security is thus very similar to common security in that nations should recognize the security interests as legitimate, and pursue peaceful coexistence.[15]

Cooperative security has come to the fore in the post-cold war period. The end of the cold war and the demise of the former Soviet Union automatically changed traditional security concepts and removed the foundations for previous strategies.[16]

Cooperative security cannot be accomplished by means of physical threats but requires that nations show mutual restraints, provide reassurances against a resort to force and enhance transparency with regard to defence policies and military postures, arms, transfers, etc. on the other hand, cooperative security is entirely compatible with those existing arrangements and regimes that have contributed to war prevention, prohibited the proliferation of nuclear, chemical, and biological weapons and long-range missiles and which have promoted arms control in general.

The UNDP Human Development Report, 1994, the first major document to use the concept, summed it up this way. "Human security is a child who did not die a disease that did not spread, a job that was not cut an ethnic tension that did not explode in violence, a dissident who was not silenced. Human security is an integrative framework. People at risk from war are also at risk from famine. Epidemics have no respect for national borders. Most development issues have to be addressed at both national and global levels. The 1994 report offered a definition: "Human Security can be said to have two main aspects. It mans, first, safety from such chronic threats as hunger, disease and repression. And second, it means protection form sudden and hurtful disruptions in the patterns of daily life whether in homes, in jobs or in communities."[17]

This early report also offered a preliminary scoping of the components of human security to be expanded to include threats in seven areas:

Economic Security: Economic security requires an assured basic income for individuals, usually from productive and remunerative work or, as a last resort from a publicly financed safety net. In this sense, only about a quarter of the world's people are presently economically secure. While the economic security problem may be more serious in developing countries, concern also arises in developed countries as well. Unemployment problems constitute an important factor underlying political tensions and ethnic violence.

Food Security: Food Security requires that all people at all times have both physical and economic access to basic food. According to the United Nations, the overall availability of food is not a problem, rather the problem often is the poor distribution of food and necessary lack of purchasing power.

Health Security: Health Security aims to guarantee a minimum protection from diseases and unhealthy lifestyles. In developing countries, the major causes of death are infections and parasitic diseases, which kill 18 million people annually. In industrialized countries, the major Killers are disease of the circulatory system, Killing 5.6 million every year. According to the United Nations, in both developing and industrial countries, threats ot health security are usually greater for poor people in rural areas, particularly children. This is mainly due to malnutrition and insufficient supply of medicine, clean water or other necessity for healthcare.

Environmental Security: Environmental Security aims to protect people from the short and long-term ravages of nature, man-made threats in nature, and deterioration of the natural environment. In developing Countries, lack of access to clean water resources is one of the greatest environmental threats. In industrial countries, one of the major threats is air pollution. Global warming, caused by the emission of greenhouse gases, is another environmental security issue.

Personal Security: Personal security aims to protect people from physical violence, whether from the state or external states, from violent individuals and sub-state actors, from domestic abuse or from predatory adults. For many people the greatest source of anxiety is crime, particularly violent crime.

Community Security: Community security aims to protect people from the loss of traditional relationships and values and from sectarian and ethnic violence. Traditional communities, particularly minority ethnic groups are often threatened. About half of the world's status have experienced some kind of inter-ethnic strife.

Political Security: Political security is concerned with whether people live in a society that honours their basic human rights. According to a survey conducted by Amnesty, political repression, systematic torture, ill-treatment or disappearance was still practiced in 112 countries. Human rights violations are most frequent during periods of political unrest. Along with repressing individuals and groups, governments may try to exercise control over ideas and information.[18]

Today's world is filled with war, terrorism turmoil and confusion, while men have created many technological inventions, they cannot be able to 'create' peace. Scientists have unleashed the power of atom but are powerless to unleash peace upon earth. The biggest danger infront of us today is that violence and science both joined hands together not only to destroy the peace of universe but also to threaten the very existence of humanity. Due to this we have lost our security and peace. Technology brings diverse people closer together in a global community it becomes increasingly important that we find ways to live together with peace in a secure world.

The search for peace and security in a world marked by extreme economic, social and cultural heterogeneity, bedeviled by self aggrandizing states which go to war against each other, states occasionally plunging the world into senseless destruction has inspired many proposals for creating one 'True world' where every individual is at peace, hence feel secure.

The whole world is faced with conflict and violence today. In fact there has been no period in history, which has not witnessed violent conflicts. But at the same time there have been sages, prophets, thinkers, religious personalities, writers, poets and sufis who always emphasized love, peace and harmony. Though both trends i.e. of violence and of peace and harmony have gone together violence and conflict remains predominant in our memory.

Notes and References

1. Kumar, Mahendra, Current Peace Research and India (New Delhi: Indra Prustha Press), 1968, p. 3.
2. Galtung, Johan, The Struggle for Peace (New Delhi, Sage Publication), 1996, pp. 50-56.
3. Webster Dictionary.

4. Morganthau, Hans, J., Politics Among Nations: The Struggle for Power and Peace (Ludhiana: Kalyani Publishers), 2007, pp. 57-70.
5. *Ibid.*
6. *Ibid.*
7. Galtung, Johan, "On the meaning of Non-violence", *Journal of Peace Research*, No. 2, pp. 228-30.
8. Human Security Centre, "What is Human Security", http:// www. human security report.
9. UNDP, Human Development Report, 1994, New York and Oxford: Oxford University Press for the UNDP, 1994, pp. 22-23.
10. *Ibid.*
11. Sabina Alkire, "A Conceptual Framework for Human Security", Centre for research on inequality, Human Security and Ethnicity, Working Paper 2, (London: University of Oxford Press), 2003.
12. *Ibid.*
13. *Ibid.*
14. King, Gary and Christopher Murray, "Rethinking Human Security", *Political Science Quarterly,* Vol. 116, No. 4, pp. 585-610.
15. *Ibid.*
16. Paris, Roland, "Human Security: Shift or Hot Air? "*International Security,* Vol. 26, No. 2, 2001, pp. 87, 102.
17. *Ibid.*
18. *Ibid.*

Peace through Education

11

MOHUA KHOSLA

Human civilization is more or less an account of war, conflicts, violence and glorification of the events and the persons who worked to bring peace and solidarity. However, the process of human development has added more to insecurity and terror of war instead of reducing it to the extent that every passing year witness the increase in the expenditure on defense and warhead preparations by every country. More developed a country is, the more preparation to counter war is. In other words, the more we strive to bring peace, the more we prepare for war. The reason for this paradoxical phenomenon is the conceptualization of *Peace* as the *absence of war* which is a negative connotation. Thus, peace is not being studied or analyzed directly for its own sake rather is studied as a subject or object of management of conflict and termination of war. World Wars I & II lead to the urgency of and subsequently the emergence of defining peace in positive sense. Galtung, a Norwegian sociologist, mathematician and the principal founder of the discipline of peace and conflict studies was the first to call for systems that would create sustainable peace and gave the concept of positive peace.

Positive peace is defined as the presence of:

- serenity, harmony, well-being
- human bonds
- shared human values (respect, acceptance, kind heartedness, equity etc.)

- strong feelings for a common humanity
- respect for universal human rights

And this is possible only through education. UNESCO also in its report *Learning: The Treasure Within* also emphasized learning to live together as one of the four pillars of education.

Mahatma Gandhi once stated, "If we are to reach real peace in this world we shall have to begin with the children." Lasting peace may depend on educating future generations into the competencies, perspectives, attitudes, values, and behavioral patterns that will enable them to build and maintain peace.

Peace is not something inert. Rather, it is an intensely active and dynamic process. It is both negative (the absence of violence) and positive (global justice) peace that peace educators strive for.

Challenging the belief that society and human beings are inherently violent is fundamental within the field of Peace Education.

War is not inevitable. Violence, rather, is learned, "essentially based on modeled behavior" of peers, families, communities, and media. And just as violence can be taught, so can peace.

Violence is expressed not only through our actions, but also through our speech and thoughts. "Most of what we call violence is in the form of action...But as long as our minds harbor violent thoughts, that incipient violence will find its way somehow into our speech and behavior." As the UNESCO Constitution famously states, "war begins in the minds of men."

The point is that violence is a choice. We might have aggressive tendencies, but how we act upon these is entirely up to us. Take the Native American Legend of Two Wolves:

> An old Cherokee is teaching his grandson about life. "A fight is going on inside me," he said to the boy. "It is a terrible fight and it is between two wolves. One is evil — he is anger, envy, sorrow, regret, greed, arrogance, self-pity, guilt, resentment, inferiority, lies, false pride, superiority, and ego." He continued, "The other is good — he is joy, peace, love, hope, serenity, humility, kindness, benevolence, empathy, generosity, truth, compassion, and faith. The same fight is going on inside you — and inside every other person, too." The grandson thought about it for a minute and then asked his

grandfather, "Which wolf will win?" The old Cherokee simply replied, "The one you feed."

Peace education is teaching the information, attitude, values and behavioural competencies needed to resolve conflicts without violence and to build and maintain mutual beneficial harmonious relationships. The ultimate goal of peace education is for individuals to be able to maintain peace among aspects of themselves (intrapersonal peace), individuals (interpersonal peace), groups (intergroup peace), and countries, societies, and cultures (international peace). To do so, peace education (among other things) needs to focus on: (a) establishing a cooperative, not a competitive relationship among all relevant parties; (b) ensuring that all relevant parties are skilled in engaging in political discourse and creative decision-making that includes an open-minded discussion of diverse views; (c) ensuring that relevant parties seek agreements that are mutually beneficial and that maximize joint outcomes; and (d) inculcating into all relevant parties the values underlying consensual peace.

Okamoto has categorized this into four types of peace education:

- *Peace education as criticism of war*: Here peace is conceptualized as the absence of war (negative peace). Content of this type includes teaching concerning the legacy of war experience, a scientific explanation of the causes of war and conditions of peace, the promotion of international understanding as a preventive to war, etc.
- *Peace education as liberation*: It conceptualized peace as liberation from poverty, ignorance, discrimination and oppression, etc. (positive peace).
- *Peace education as a learning process*: In this type, peace education is grasped as a learning process towards inter-personal maturity on the basis o the unity between theory and practice on the one hand and a critical understanding of history and society on the other.
- *Peace education as life-style movements*: It rests upon the realization that warfare and war preparations are intimately tied to the fact that the over-production and extravagance of the nations at the center have been gained at the expense of the wealth and development of nations

at the periphery. We can refer to a standard of values emphasizing a simple life, human scale, self-determination, ecological awareness and personal growth.

Peace education is not simply a subject, it is a holistic approach, a way of thinking. It is comprised of multiple sub-fields in which scholars and practitioners work, but often are not considered part of peace education. These sub-fields such as global security and human rights education, have often developed in their own right and hence are referred to here as "co-disciplines" of peace education which includes:

1. Human Rights Education
2. Developmental Education
3. Disarmament Education
4. Environment Education
5. Moral Education
6. Education for Sustainable Development
7. Education for International Understanding
8. Inclusive Education
9. Education for Conflict Resolution
10. Life Skills Education
11. Social Justice Education
12. Education for Liberation and Empowerment, etc.

VALUES AND ATTITUDES REQUIRED FOR PEACE EDUCATION

Values and attitudes underpin peace education and need to be addressed through the curriculum and the whole school which are as follows:

i. Respect for others regardless of race, gender, age, nationality, class, sexuality, appearance, political or religious belief, physical or mental ability
ii. Empathy—a willingness to understand the views of others from their standpoint
iii. A belief that individuals and groups of people can make for positive change
iv. Self esteem—accepting the intrinsic value of oneself
v. Commitment to social justice, equity and nonviolence

vi. Concern for the environment and understanding of our place in the eco-system

vii. Commitment to equality

The primary purpose of peace education should therefore be to build people's capacities to recognize, confront, and transform the culture of violence. "Central to such a challenge is providing students with the skills, knowledge, and authority they need to inquire and act upon what it means to live in a substantive democracy...to fight deeply rooted injustices in a society and world founded on systematic economic, racial, and gendered inequalities." Such social change cannot be forced upon people.

Peace education should therefore be student centered a process of mutual learning among students and educator. However, it faces many external challenges posed by society, the school environment, and students themselves. The greatest challenge for peace educators, however, is to "be the peace they preach." This cannot be just an intellectual enterprise. Teaching peace must involve a "holy war in the soul", a searching within for the things you are trying to teach. Wouldn't it be hypocritical to teach peace without an honest attempt to achieve it yourself? As Del Vasto states, "before you can spread peace on earth, you must have brought it into your own home, and there can be no peace in your home if there is none in your heart." It is no longer sufficient to think that events are isolated and that one's actions do not affect others. It is high time to realize and accept that "everything that happens is everybody's concern and everybody's responsibility." Then only we can make peace education effective and sustainable, aiming to find root cause of each problem rather than applying a 'BAND-AID' solution that will address only the surface. If taken in right perspective PEACE EDUCATION can provide answer to all problems—from injustice to poverty, from personal anxiety to interpersonal conflicts, from neighborhood misunderstanding to international tension.

References

Bajaj, Monisha and Chiu, Belinda (2009). Education for Sustainable Development as Peace Education. Peace & Change, 34(4).

Delors, Jacques. Learning: The Treasure Within. UNESCO.

Galtung, Johan (1969). Violence, Peace and Peace Research, *Journal of Peace Research*, 6(3): 167-91.

Mitina, Valentino (1994). "New Thinking: Its Application for a New Learning," in *Learning Peace: The Promise of Ecological and Cooperative Education,* ed.

Betty Reardon and Eva Norland, New York: State University of New York Press, 50.

Okamoto, Mitsuo. 1984. Peace Research and Peace Education: What is Peace Education in the New Light of Peace Research? *Ghandi Marg*, 6(4,5), 217-28.

Reardon, Betty (1988). Comprehensive Peace Education. New York: Teachers College Press.

Thoresen, Victoria W. (2011). Learning to Live Together Education for Sustainable Living Policies and practices from around the world. *Partnership for Education and Research about Responsible Living*. Hedmark University College, Norway Photo Credits: Colourbox.

UNESCO, "Education for Sustainable Development," http://portal.unesco.org/education/en/ev.phpURL_ID=23279&URL_DO=DO_TOPIC&URL_SECTION=201.html.

Wenden, Anita (2002). Education for a Culture of Peace. Earth and Peace Education Associates International (2002). Retrieved from http://www.globalepe.org/resources.html.

Non-Violence in Modern Times 12

WASEEM SAEED

It is rightly said that Mahatma Gandhi was the saviour of souls and not the wrecker of civilizations. He came to build and not to destroy. His ideals were concord in place of discord, peace and cooperation in place of conflicts and tensions and progress in place of retrogression. According to Gandhi, man is potentially perfect, basically good, and inherently capable of truthful and non-violent conduct and behaviour in all situations and in all departments of life. In the words of Gandhi, "I have found that life persists in the midst of destruction and therefore there must be a higher law than that of destruction and that higher law is the law of nonviolence".[1]

The most fundamental and crucial concept in Gandhian thought is Satya or truth from which is derived Ahimsa or nonviolence. Satya and Ahimsa are so losely interrelated that it is practically impossible to disentangle and separate them and they are like the two sides of a coin. As self-conscious and rational beings, we are fully aware of moral values like truth and nonviolence, justice and righteousness and we are also intrinsically aware of the fact that forces of truth and justice will always triumph over forces of falsehood and injustice. The word Ahimsa literally means non-injury and non-killing and in a wider sense harmlessness and free from hostile thoughts, words and actions. As early as 1916, Gandhi distinguished between the negative and positive meanings of Ahimsa. In its negative form, it means not injuring any living being—whether by body or mind. In its positive form, Ahimsa means the largest measure of love and compassion towards all the living creatures. A votary of Ahimsa must love his enemy without any hatred or ill-will and the principle to be followed is 'hate evil and not the evil-doer.' It is no non-violence, if we merely love those that love us. On the other hand, it is non-violence, when we love those that hate us.

Long before the Christians thought about loving their enemies, the Hindus chanted hymns of praise to the spiritual oneness and unity of all lives in this world. These hymns clearly indicate great respect and reverence for life, which our Hindu tradition defines as Ahimsa or refusal to do any harm to life. More than five hundred years before the birth of Jesus Christ, Lord Buddha declared: "Let every person overcome angel by love, let him overcome evil by good, let him overcome the greedy by liberality, the liar by truth". In Dhammapada, we have the golden rule of conduct and action. "Hatred does not cease by hatred at any time. Hatred ceases by love and nonviolence." Socrates, in his attitude towards the Greek State, reminded his friends that those who practised nonviolence in an unexamind life is not worth living. Nonviolence is precisely this appeal to examine the meaning of life in the ultimate sense, which in turn demands a dynamic response to every new situation. In our daily lives, all thinking persons are confronted with the puzzling question, when they choose their course of action, what will be the consequences not only for themselves, but also for their fellowmen and for the society and, above all, what must be the appropriate motives for their actions. Our response to these questions may involve commitment to nonviolence, which may be interpreted as our strong beliefs or convictions on our tactics to solve our problems or strategies to overcome our difficulties.

In the immortal words of Gandhi, "man as animal is violent, but as spirit is nonviolent. Either he progresses towards Ahimsa or rushes to his doom".[1] Acting nonviolently is demonstrating or vindicating justice and truth and an advocate of nonviolence will never retreat in cowardice in any situation. Gandhi tells us: "My nonviolence does not admit of running away from danger and leaving dear ones unprotected. I can only prefer violence to cowardice. I can no more preach nonviolence to a coward than I can tempt a blind man to enjoy beautiful sence."[2] In short, nonviolence is the summit of bravery. We are all aware that in modern times, violence ranges from brutal physical and mental destructiveness to more civilized uses of force. A familar model of nonviolence is the friendly persuasion used by the Quakers in their historical efforts to find peaceful solutions to violent problems and their unique response to the violence of Vietnam war was to sail into Hanoi's harbour with a shipment of medical supplies.

In modern times, in order to acieve harmony between the individual and the society and among the nations, it is necessary according to Gandhi, to achieve harmony within oneself and with nature and with cosmos. If men and women are truthful, honest and nonviolent in their daily lives, as individuals and in their personal relationships with their fellow citizens, others will also be truthful, honest and nonviolent as members of the society. For example, promises are made in one's circle or in their society to keep the same and they will have moral value, when those promises are followed. On the other hand, when promises are made to be broken at the next opportunity, promises will have no moral value and the members in the circle or in the society will completely lose faith in promises and there will be utter confusion, chaos and disharmony in such a society. Further, we must recognize any form of violence—mental, verbal and physical—as a direct violation of (he indivisible and irrevocable bond of unity that is inherent among us, under the universal law of material and moral principles of cause and effect. So, our primary task must be to alter our attitude of mind and bring about change of heart, rather than merely tamper with our external conditions and surroundings. The great disparity between belief and profession, between profession and practice retard and counteract the good results. Nonviolent and truthful life can be made effective, when the causes of violence and factors of untruth that arise out of violations of truth, have ceased to operate. Similarly, conflicts and tensions can be resolved, when we refrain from forcing our personal prejudices, opinions and interests on others. Let us remember that the true religious attitude means voluntary acceptance and fulfillment of one's duties and true religious spirit implies observance of one's duties, not out of fear of penal sanctions, but born from a sense of inner compulsiveness, generated by comparison and love for human beings, i.e. the path of truth and nonviolence. The theory of nonviolence is based on the assumption that divinity that resides in all individuals is the same, -which leads to respect for all religions. Gandhi believed in the unity of life, oneness of God and in the indivisibility of mankind. Further, he believed in the highly educative and transforming influence of personal example. Indeed ! His life is his message to his followers. It is very often asked whether Gandhi wanted to abolish violence or reduce it. He wanted both. He wanted to reduce violence and also vanquish violence in all departments of life. This stupendous and gigantic task involves an infinitely gradual process. He did not hope that violence would disappear overnight in the world—rather he expected conditions to be created for violence to be eschewed as quickly as possible. Thus, in Gandhi we have simultaneously an idealist, who presents the absolute ideal of nonviolence and a pragmatist or a practical man, who recognized that one must struggle against violence and also change world conditions in such a way that violence becomes less and less conceivable. In modern times, we must try our best to change the general situation and atmosphere of humanity slowly and steadily, so that the universal and eternal message of nonviolence begins to be recognized and heeded. Nonviolence does not mean surrender to evil or unjust forces nor does nonviolent struggle mean compromise with violence. This clearly indicates that Gandhi was in favour of struggles and all struggles involve the use of proper weapons strong enough to achieve the desired goals. Then it is necessary to manifest moral strength through nonviolence by acting and influencing others by means other than physical force.

Dr. Thomas Walz, Professor of social work in the University of Iowa, communicates a new philosophy of nonviolent management to be introduced into the education of future administrators and the managers and this training must include preparation in human development as opposed to the present training in the technology of product development. In nonviolent management, we must redesign our organizations to human scale, since large-scale organizations necessarily produce problems that tend towards violence. Dr. Thomas Walz endorses the concept of Sarvodaya, which offers a blueprint towards nonviolent approach towards large-scale organization and management, incorporating the notion of human development and reorganising social institutions at human scale. We may describe Sarvodaya as the totality or the grand synthesis of Gandhian thought in theory and in practice. In modern times, Sarvodaya based on Truth and Nonviolence is acclaimed as a dynamic social philosophy, which can usher in the advent of a radically transformed, casteless and classless societies all over the world. In the Sarvodaya social order, there will be no place for the party system and consequently no struggle for power and the future society will be a form of polity very different from the politics of socialism and communism and capitalism. Indeed, Gandhi's Sarvodaya project is a model for every society all over the world and is intensely humanist-oriented towards the needs of the community as a whole and paves the way to establish a new world order for peace, progress and prosperity. Gandhi was perhaps the first and foremost in the modern world to apply the same code of conduct based on truth and nonviolence both to the personal life of any individual and to the public life of communities and nations. In fact, Gandhi wore no masks, nor did he ever disguise himself. Underlying his approach to life and world problems was his great and abiding faith in God, truth and nonviolence, unity of life and, above all, unity of mankind.

We see conflicts and tensions all around us in the world and our modern civilization is at crossroads. We also find that conflicts are regular features in the history of human race. What is surprising and remarkable is that the methods adopted and followed to end such conflicts have generally failed or produced greater conflicts. Gandhi pointed out the new and dynamic path of nonviolence to end conflicts and to shape our thoughts and actions. In this new approach, he added a new dimension to nonviolence and thus converted a passive principle into a dynamic doctrine of Satyagraha to fight against injstice, exploitation and different other forms of violence. In Gandhian thought, creative resolution of conflicts—an expression coined by Joan V. Bondurant—is possible, when violent relationship is transformed into a nonviolent one and the energies of opponents are integrated to achieve higher good. In the opinion of Gandhi, it is the faulty system, which binds the opposing parties to hostile relation. So, the techniques must involve ways and means to change the system itself in a nonviolent manner. Bondurant calls the mechanism of self-suffering as a shock-therapy on the opponent[3] and Jacques Maritain sees in it Gandhi's real genius. Further, nonviolence implies complete self-purification and is always superior to violence and the power at the disposal of a nonviolent person is always greater than that of a violent person and the ultimate end of nonviolence is definite victory, which implies that the followers of ahimsa never aim at defeating anybody, but aim at achieving desirable results. Gandhi's appeal to nonviolence was ultimately an appeal to the conscience and the reason of the individual and an affirmation of the dignity and divinity of the human personality, as well as the glory of the purity of means.[4] To quote Gandhi: "I have often said that if one takes care of the means, the ends will take care of itself and nonviolence is the means." Means and end, in Gandhian thought, are distinguishable only temporarily, since both means and ends partake in a continuous process. In the final analysis, the concept of nonviolence becomes both the means and the end and the terms become convertible. Gandhi felt that nonviolent struggle had to be carried beyond the frontiers of India. In his view, nonviolent struggle should be the only weapon of struggle both at the national and at the international levels. Martin Luther King, Jr., describes in *Stride Towards Freedom,* six basic principles in the philosophy of nonviolent resistance: (i) Nonviolent resistance is not a method for cowards. It is an active nonviolent resistance to evil and seeks to change the mind of his opponent, (ii) An atmosphere of tragic bitterness and hatred is the result of violence and not that of nonviolence. A nonviolent resister does not seek to humiliate his opponent, but attempts to win his friendship and understanding. (iii) Nonviolent resistance is an attack directed against the forces of evil and injustice, rather than against persons, who happen to perform evil and unjust acts. (iv) Nonviolent resistance is the willingness to accept suffering without retaliation, since self-suffering has a powerful educational and transforming influence on man. (v) Nonviolent resistance avoids external, physical, internal, emotional, and spiritual violence, (vi) The resistor refuses to hate his opponent or to become involved in hate campaign and this attitude is possible on account of ethic of love and compassion as centre of all actions.[5]

Gandhi believed that nonviolence is a spiritual force or soul force. In the words of Gandhi, "nonviolence is the only thing that the atom bomb or nuclear missiles cannot destory. Unless the world adopts nonviolence, it will spell, certain suicide for mankind."[6] In addition to the path of nonviolence, Gandhi pleaded that the root causes of wars, exploitation and injustice must end, if there is to be permanent peace on the earth. U Thant, on the opening day of the Gandhi Centenary Year in October 1968, acknowledged that the Charter of the United Nations is founded on the principles and ideals propounded by Gandhi. MacArthur observed that there was no future for mankind unless nations turned away from war and violence and accepted the way of Gandhi the path of truth and nonviolence. According to Gandhi, truth and nonviolence are not analytical concepts, but synthetic ones. For Gandhi, nonviolence and truth are one whole, totality or Gestalt and in his opinion, truth incarnates as love and love translates itself into action and incarnates as nonviolence. Above all, Gandhi placed so much importance on truth and nonviolence that they are bound to become absolute essentials for humanity. In modern times, we observe that great economic inequalities among different nations are increasrog and the racist regime in South Africa continues to pursue its policies of discrimination and aparthied. It is only today, we can truly appreciate the vision and foresight of Gandhi, when he warned us of the threats that these inequalities and injustices hold for the progress of humanity. Therefore, the great revolutionary task of Gandhi is not finished. It calls for new and dynamic efforts for humanity to be rid of fear, hatred and for men to be re-educated in the use of nonviolent methods, so that societies all over the world may be reformed on the basis of the principles of equality, freedom, justice, truth and nonviolence. Today, after decolonization, the world is politically and economically a relatively open system, and acts of violence are so many and manifold that in addition to localized nonviolent resistance, solidarity of nonviolent resisters in all parts of the world, may alert public of opinion—regional or international-to solve the problems of organising peace, security and stability.[7]

Men are the only animals that destroy their own kind so mercilessly it is not only inhuman but sub-human and men alone use distant weaponry for mass destruction. Disarmament means the path of nonviolence. So, following the path of nonviolence, all the nations of the world must renounce violence and there must be global or total disarmament. As a fist step to avoid nuclear perils and dangers, Gandhi suggested unilateral disarmament or establishing nuclear-free zones at strategic and sensitive zones. Since the problems of the world have grown so enormous and gigantic, they can be solved through a global perspective and through a vision and approach that encompasses the whole world. This dynamic approach and vision can be offered only by men of science and spirituality, creative thinkers and humanists, who recognise no frontiers of race, colour creed or nationality. The men of science and spirituality have to come together and forge a new communion and work together to create a new global outlook for global disarmament.[8]

If today the world has a number of problems that seem to be very complicated and insoluble, it is because, we are in an age of disbelief, mistrust, suspicion and violent attitudes towards those problems. So, the need of the modern times is change in our attitudes and to develop supreme faith in truth and nonviolence, divine love and compassion. To raise the question like the relevance of Gandhi's teachings and techniques is like asking the question: "What is the relevance of the sun to the solar system?" Gandhi's teachings and techniques arc for endless time or for eternity and he gave us the priceless gifts of self-respect and the sense of identity with the brotherhood of humanity and the matchless weapon of Satyagraha, more powerful and mightier than the hydrogen bomb or the nuclear bomb. Above all, Gandhi dealt with problems that are timeless and universal, since they spring from weaknesses of human nature and human society and the great solutions be found for them were based on eternal values and virtues and their relevance is also timeless and universal. By his emphasis on truth and nonviolence and purity of means in all the departments of life, he stressed the aspirations and ideals of humanity of all ages and heralded the dawn of spiritual epoch in human history. Late Acharya Vinoba Bhave pronounced that the days of religion and politics were over and science and spirituality would rule the minds of mankind.

What we require today is the harmonious blending or creative synthesis of the results of modern science and technology and spiritual values and cultivation and promotion of positive human values like truth and nonviolence, love and compassion, togetherness and brotherhood of humanity leading to world federation and everlasting peace on the earth.

Notes and References

1. *Ibid.*, p. 87.
2. *Ibid.*, p. 102.
3. Joan V. Bondurant, Conquest of Violence.
4. Anand T. Hingorani (ed.), The Art of Living, p. 47.
5. Martin Luther King, Jr., Stride Towards Freedom, pp. 81-86.
6. Thomas Kiernan, The Wisdom of Gandhi.
7. Timothy Leary, Alternative to Violence.
8. R.R. Diwakar and Mahendra Agarwal, Vinoba: The Spiritual Revolutionary.

Towards a Peaceful Society

13

ANITA RATHORE

The late Professor Quincy Wright convincingly showed in his monumental work. *The Study of War*,[1] that conflicts and wars were menacingly frequent. During this period from 1484 to 1945, according to Wright, there were 278 wars spread over all the continents. That wars cause a lot of misery both to the individual and the society as a whole is well known. We are told, for example, that the total number of lives lost during the two World Wars (1914-18 and 1939-45) was 26 million military personnel and 64 million civilians.[2] This does not take into account the sufferings of the injured, the widowed and orphaned nor the total disruption of life in general. Towards the end of the Second World War a new and very destructive weapon, namely the Atom Bomb, was used to destroy completely the twin cities of Hiroshima and Nagasaki in Japan.

We may at this stage ask ourselves the question why religions such as Hinduism, Buddhism, Christianity, Islam, and Sikhism were not able to secure such values as universal brotherhood, love and peace leading to the elimination of war. We have no space here to answer this question in detail : perhaps the inability of religions to prevent war and other conflicts was due to the fact that these religions were partial in the sense that followers of any one of them numbered only a fraction of the world's population.

The remarkable development of science and technology during the last two centuries has further contributed to the misery caused by wars. This development has had two contradictory results. On the one hand, it has brought about great improvement in living standards everywhere. Unprecedented advancement in transport and communication, discovery of new varieties of crops and fertilizers, new time-saving and labour-saving industrial methods and the like have been made. On the other hand, development of science and technology has also led to the invention of destructive weapons, which can annihilate mankind from the very face of the earth.

Mankind is at the crossroads of history. It may, by outlawing war, choose the path of social progress and high living standards and abolish poverty, ignorance and disease or by failing to take effective steps to outlaw war continue to face social misery and/or self-destruction. Where do we go from here?

ACCEPTANCE OF HUMANISM : A POSSIBLE ANSWER

It appears to us that the adoption of Humanism as a way of life by all the peoples of the world is the only way out of the dangerous situation. Humanism means respect for man as man and not only because of his individual achievements. A Shakespeare, a Winston Churchill, an Einstein and a Mahatma Gandhi have to be respected as men even if one had not written excellent dramas, another was not a great statesman, the third was not a great scientist and the fourth had not been an apostle of nonviolence, truth and peace. The essence of the humanist view is the importance placed on the human being, the individual as the centre of all human activity and aspirations. A passage from Sri Aurobindo's.

IDEAL OF HUMAN UNITY DESCRIBES HUMANISM

The fundamental idea of Humanism is that mankind is the godhead to be worshipped and served by man and that the respect, the service, the progress of the human being and human life are the chief duty and chief aims of the human spirit. No other idol, neither the nation, the State, family nor anything else ought to take its place; they are only worthy of respect so far as they are images of the human spirit and enshrine its presence and aid its self manifestation. But where the cult of these idols seeks to usurp the place of the spirit and makes demands inconsistent with its service; they should be put aside. No injunctions of old creeds, religious, political, social or cultural, are valid when they go against its claims.[3]

Mahatma Gandhi had said: "I look upon an increase of the power of the state with the greatest fear, because, although while apparently doing good by minimising exploitation, it does the greatest harm to mankind by destroying individuality which lies at the root of all progress."[4]

Modern Indian writers, like M.N. Roy, also agreed that new Humanism emphasises the fact that "man is the maker of his world—man as a thinking being, and he can be so only as an individual." The brain which is the instrument of thought, he said, is individually owned, and cannot be possessed collectively.[5] This new Humanism, Roy strongly believed, had to be interrelated with science in order to further the progress of civilization. For, "in the past also, Humanism proclaimed the sovereignty of man. But man remained unexplained, and speculation about the essence of man led to mysticism and revival of religion. Thus Humanism defeated itself."[6] Scientific knowledge, however, had freed it from mystic and metaphysical fallacies about the essence of man, which in the past had "led to the subordination of man to imaginary forces beyond his comprehension."[7]

It is noteworthy that some states have adopted Humanism as basic to their national programmes. Foremost in this regard is Zambia, whose interpretation of Humanism into action is based on a mancentred society and thus all its development plans are man-oriented. The individual is central to all its policies, whether in the rural or the urban areas. From this would follow the well-being of the whole society. In a speech outlining his Party's policies. President Kaunda highlighted the importance of the individual in the society, for, he reasoned "we cannot expect a country to be better than its own individuals; for, a country is what its individuals make it." This high value placed on man himself enhances not only his role as a human being, but also that which he plays and contributes to society and the world. This value and recognition is the essence of humanism. Humanism is a compound of six major principles, namely, nonviolence, equality, concern for others, freedom, non-exploitation and cooperation. An elaboration of these principles follows.

PRINCIPLES OF HUMANISM

Nonviolence

The role of nonviolence in Humanism should be clear from

the fact that without protectirg the life and person of the individual, the latter cannot act in the way he desires. The first implication of nonviolence is the protection of the life and person of the individual. The second implication is that whatever be the nature of the individual's crime, capital punishment must not be imposed on him; For, the individual cannot be promoted if the State itself takes away the life of the individual. Although capital punishment has been abolished in most states of Western Europe including Britain (except France, Greece and Spain, and in most states of Latin America), it is still retained in the United States, Canada, Africa, most Asian States, Australia, Eastern Europe and the Balkans. However, a report issued by the United Nations in 1962, showed that there was a growing tendency among nations to reduce the number of crimes under which capital punishment could be imposed.[8] Several States, including India, hesitate to abolish capital punishment on the ground that in underdeveloped countries capital punishment cannot be avoided without the risk of encouraging such heinous crimes as murder or abetment of murder. While admitting this, one can only say that in such a situation the principle of nonviolence so essential to; remote humanism required protection and nurturing in a more carefully.

It will be useful at this stage to refer to Mahatma Gandhi's view on nonviolence. Mahatma Gandhi brought nonviolence to the level of collective action in the Indian National Movement. But for Mahatma Gandhi, non-violence in collective action was more than an instrument of political action. It was a distinct way of life. He said: "The religion of nonviolence is not meant merely for the rishis and saints. It is meant for the common people as well. Nonviolence is the law of our species as violence is the law of the brute. The spirit lies dormant in the brute and he knows no law but that of physical might. The dignity of man requires obedience to a higher law—to the strength of the spirit."[9] Opposing war, he held that "science of war leads one to dictatorship pure and simple. Science of nonviolence alone can lead one to pure democracy. Nonviolence which could be practised individually and collectively was not just a negative quality but a positive force of love and patience born out of the conviction that human beings can be persuaded and morally converted so as to make them act in the way of truth and righteousness. It is synonymous with truth and at the heart of all religions."

One question may be asked in connection with the practice of nonviolence if ociety involved two things. "The first is an attitude of mind, an attitude of respect and equality towards other fellows. The second is a social organization free from rigid social barriers. Democracy is incompatible and inconsistent with isolation and exclusiveness, resulting in the distinction between the privileged and the unprivileged."[10] Fundamental rights, he felt, were meaningless unless these were accompanied by "social and moral conscience of society."[11]

Equality is not similarity, nor can it be forced upon, implying some kind of regimentation. As Vinoba Bhave observed, equality should be "tempered with discrimination." Citing an example, he said, a mother does not feed her children on the basis of mathematical equality but according to the needs of each child. Every child, however, should have the opportunity to be fed. In a humanist society it is fundamental that harmony among the people be promoted through adequate opportunities for each person to develop fully, according to his or her own needs.

CONCERN FOR OTHERS

If nonviolence and equality are the two basic principles of humanism, concern for others comes very close to both. Concern for others means that an individual must respect the rights of others and be as unselfish as he can. This is implicit in society. We cannot, however, assert that an individual must be entirely unselfish because he has to protect his own interests as well. If he does not protect his own interests, who will protect them? What is meant by concern for others is that the individual must show some consideration for the interests of others. Such consideration leads to contentment and harmony in society.

In a world full of ignorance and disease, all citizens are morally bound to do what they can to eradicate them. Poverty is rampant in many parts of the world; and apart from government action and voluntary associations, individual help is also essential to eliminate poverty.

While there are many views on human nature, it would be true to say that concern for others or unselfishness is part of human nature. While Hobbes held that the life of man is "solitary, poor, nasty, brutish and short", this view has been vigorously challenged by other writers. Moreover, history shows that there has been unselfish action by many individuals, organisations and governments. Indeed, the two words—"charity" and "sacrifice"—remind us that unselfishness is also an important element in human nature.

Freedom

The term "freedom" is used in two senses. First, national freedom, which of course implies preservation of the independence and the sovereignty of the State; second, individual freedom, which means that the individual has various rights such as freedom of speech, freedom of the press, religious freedom of association and freedom to do what he thinks best for himself, provided he does not interfere with the freedom of others. In the context of our discussion on Humanism, the second connotation is more relevant. In this context, the two definitions of freedom, one negative and the other positive, are important. In the negative sense, freedom implies absence of restraint by government on those conditions which are necessary for the development of the individual's personality. The positive aspect of freedom emphasised by the State of those opportunities which are essential for self-development. To take one example, everyone will consider it essential in an underdeveloped State to enact legislation on compulsory education up to 14 or 15 years of age. The oft-repeated saying that "government is best which govern least" has to be interpreted in the sense that such legislation is necessary for an individual to develop his personality.

In humanism, the required freedom is important because the individual is the centre round whom all activities of the State must revolve. Usually, freedom of the individual is protected by the essential freedoms incorporated in a written declaration of rights in the constitution. This holds good, for example, both in India and the United States of America. The advantage of this is that the Judiciary can interpret the constitution to safeguard freedom in an appropriate manner. Freedom of speech, the press, association, religion, political rights such as the right to vote and the right to stand as a candidate for election to the legislature and the freedom to pursue the vocation which the citizen chooses are the essential elements of individual freedom. From the economic point of view, the right to property is invariably included in the declaration.

Non-exploitation

Exploitation is the using of one person's weakness by another for his or her personal advantage. Such exploitation may take several forms —political, economic, and social. Political exploitation occurs when a ruling political group oppresses the poor for personal advantage of the members of the ruling group. The obvious example of such exploitation is the oppression of the African majority by the White minority group in South Africa.

Now we pass on to economic exploitation. Here, we may refer to the exploitation of the poor workers by the capitalists by employing the workers in factories, paying them inadequate wages, by maintaining long hours of work, by employing children in the factories under hazardous conditions of work. Some African leaders like President Kaunda and Julius Nyrere believe that capitalism represents the chief source of exploitation as its selfish and acquisitive tendencies create disparities among different sections of people.

Social oppression or exploitation takes place when the caste Hindus, for example, practise untouchability even after the Constitution of India clearly lays down that untouchability must not be practised. The late B.R. Ambedkar referred to the plight of even highly paid officers in Baroda who could not be approached by caste Hindu subordinates; these subordinate employees threw files from their desks to the senior officers who were sitting say some ten yards away from them. Even worse than untouchability is unapproachability. In Kerala, some years ago, the depressed classes (now called Harijans) were prevented by the caste Hindus from entering villages where they lived. We can recollect the noise made by the poor depressed classes if they wanted anything from the village. Exploitation of man by man, as illustrated above, lowers the dignity of the individual and makes him unhappy. In a humanist society, any form of exploitation must be avoided. Leaders of society have to do their best to prevent such exploitation.

Cooperation

Cooperation is implicit in social organisations. No State can function properly without the active co-operation of its people. The interdependence of individuals in society cannot be ignored if only because the skills of each vary from one to another. In his interpretation of humanism in action, President Kaunda of Zambia gives us a very interesting picture of the traditional society in which cooperation was practised. People then actively co-operated with each other from the craddle to the grave. They not only enjoyed a democratic way of life but also cooperated in social and economic fields; for instance, at birth, the newborn was received by a number of carefully selected women who would also take care of the mother. The baby would then be the responsibility of not only the parents and relatives but also of the society as a whole. Its growth and education would be the responsibility of the elders in society who were respected for their wisdom. During sickness, society took care of those so afflicted. Economic organisation was clearly defined and it was important from the individual as also from the communal aspect. Each individual worked hard not only for himself and his family but also for the community. Resources, efforts and skills were often pooled for the general well-being and advancement. Construction of houses was a communal effort, with men and women contributing their labour for houses to be owned by different individuals. So too with the making of gardens which the community would co-operate to develop, although these gardens would be individually owned, and crops individually stored. The traditional society recognised the importance of a mutual-aid society.

In India, too, one ran note various aspects of cooperation which were prevalent in traditional society. In the State of Kerala, for instance, during festivals, the neighbours cooperated in preparing various dishes voluntarily. On the occasion of Lord Krishna's birth, which according to tradition took place at midnight, it was the custom for people to keep vigil until the auspicious moment. Young girls of the village would go around to the neighbors to collect oil to keep the lamps burning. Indeed such mutual aid in the celebration of religious festivals is quite common in all parts of the world. Cooperation might have been easy in the traditional society because it was compact, and one neighbour knew the other. In today's world, such cooperation may not be forthcoming because villages have become larger in size and the traditional family system has broken down.

In the international field also, cooperation is essential, because of interdependence of States. The United Nations, in fact, provides for such cooperation not only politically, but in every aspect of development through its various specialised agencies.

HURDLES TO BE OVERCOME

There are, however, hurdles to be crossed before the aim can be realized.

Opposition from the established religions must be anticipated, though such opposition cannot be justified because Humanism does not interfere with the religious belief of any group. It is concerned with the way of life and not with religion. However, opposition from religious groups may come because acceptance of Humanism by the whole world may overshadow the existing religions and their followers. This should warn us that people of the world must be fully educated in the tasic principles of Humanism and also that the Humanists must be slow in establishing such a society. In this regard governments and non-governmental organisations should make full use of the media to advertise and educate peoples all over the globe. An extraordinary situation needs an extraordinary remedy and therefore those who support Humanism must go slow in introducing it. Centuries may lapse before this becomes a reality.

A second hurdle is that millions of people, more especially in the underdeveloped countries, are illiterate. According to available statistics, over 46 millions[12] of people are at present illiterate, i.e. they do not know how to read and write. Therefore, how the message of Humanism can reach them has to be thought carefully.

A third hurdle is, if violence is abolished, a question may be asked how should governments deal with those who break the law, since by definition they have no access to weapons. This is a very difficult question and we have no ready answer for it.

NOTES AND REFERENCES

1. Quincy Wright, The Study of War, Chicago, University of Chicago Press, 1965.
2. David L. Sills, ed., International Encyclopaedia of the Social Sciences, Vol. 16, Washington, The Macmillan Company, 1968, p. 458.
3. A. Appadorai, Documentation on Political Thought in Modern India, Vol. II, Bombay, Oxford University Press, 1967, p. 777.
4. *Ibid.*, p. 140.
5. M.N. Roy, Romanticism and Revolution, Vol. 2, Calcutta, 1965.
6. *Ibid.*, pp. 307-08.

7. *Ibid.*
8. David L. Sills, ed., International Encyclopedia of the Social Sciences, Vol. 2. *op. cit.*, pp. 292-93.
9. *Young India*, 4 August 1920.
10. A. Appadorai, Documentation on Political Thought in Modern India, Vol. I, *op. cit.*, pp. 12, 176.
11. *Ibid.*, p. 127.
12. U.N. Statistical Yearbook, 1983-84.

Peace Studies

A Feminist Perspective

14

PREETI SINGH

With the increasing number of inter-state and intra-state conflicts peace studies has become one of the most important areas of social science researches. The increasing number of conflicts and its negative impact on the quality of life and development of the nation has proved that through war and conflict goal of prosperity cannot be achieved. The negative relation between violent conflict and social prosperity has made it necessary for the social scientists to search for an alternative paradigm. Emergence of peace studies is a step in this direction. For a long time, peace is misconceived as mere absence of war but gradually it has been proved that peace is not mere opposite to war or conflict, therefore what is needed is not only removal of conflicts but also eradication of the very root of conflicts. If one looks for the root of conflict, he/she would find that the very reason behind any conflict or war is basically injustice and feeling of deprivation whether actual, imaginative or constructed. Whenever a community, a nation or group is denied justice community, a nation or group is denied justice or it feels that justice has been denied to it, it's this feeling of dissatisfaction leads to unrest which ultimately may result in conflict. Thus, in order to establish peace what is needed is a system based on justice. However, the term justice is so ambiguous that it is very difficult to define what a just system means to be because what is justice for one can be injustice for the other. However, here when I use the term justice, without going in philosophical debate on the meaning of justice, I accept the commonsense understanding of the term justice, according to which any system can be addressed as a just system if it does not deprive any individual or group from its due share in the social, economic, culture and political good. In other words, the system must not be based on any kind of discrimination. To make it little more precise it can be said that peace demands a just, democratic, transparent and egalitarian social system.

When seen from such broader perspective then gender justice seems to be an integral part of the notion of peace. A society where half of the population is subjected to inhumane treatment cannot ever be called peaceful. It would not be wrong to propose that the relation between women's status and peace is that of reciprocity. On the one hand, women can have their own space only in a peaceful society, on the other only that society can be called peaceful where women get their due share in social, economic, political and cultural capital.

Perhaps due to this significant relation between women and peace, the feminist perspective is considered as one of the most dominates perspectives in the contemporary discourse on peace. Researchers in the field of peace studies have started accepting that any discourse on peace would remain incomplete if feminist perspective is not taken into account. Here, when I claim that inclusion of women's perspective in peace studies is a recent development, I do not mean that women were absent in the earlier discourse on peace. I only want to submit that though women were there but woman's perspective was absent there. The approach was of adding women to the existing peace discourse but not of including their perspective. It can be said that the traditional discourse on peace was based on latent exclusion of women. To further explain the point, it cannot be denied that women had been always there in the war and peace literature but portrayed only as victims. In the process of seeing women only as victims of wars and conflicts, women's agency of peace has not been given due recognition. But roles played by women in conflict ridden and post conflict societies are evidence of woman's agency of peace. There is no denial of the fact that is the most valuable victims during the wars and conflict situations but at the same time it must be accepted that they are not only victims. Thus, the relation between women and peace is multilayered which seeks to be investigated in order to get a comprehensive and broader understanding of peace.

The notion of peace is widely discussed by the social scientists but still the researchers have not reached to consensus on the exact meaning of the term. Though peace is seen by all as the ideal state of any society but there is a big debate on the question that what kind of society this would be? Whether this would be a society free from violent conflicts? or would this be a society where there shall not be any discrimination on the basis of caste, class, race, gender, ethnicity, nationality and so on? or would this be a society where there shall not be any discrimination on the basis of caste, class, race, gender, ethnicity, nationality and so on? or would this be a society where every and group of individuals would get their due share in the socio-economic, cultural and political system and would be entitled to lead a dignified life?

These questions refer to the ambiguity of the term peace. J. Galtung's notions of negative peace and positive peace[1] can help us in understanding the term in a broader context. The negative notice of peace conceives peace as mere 'the end or absence of widespread violent conflict'. If one goes by this limited meaning of peace then a society based on domination and unequal relations between ethic-religious communities, classes, and sexes can be labeled as peaceful until this inequality and domination get culminated into violent conflicts. In contrast to this limited notion of peace, the notion of positive peace conceives peace as not mere absence of violent conflict but as absence of structures of violence and relations of domination and inequality. According to this notion of positive peace, a society in order to be called a peaceful society should have an active and egalitarian civil society, inclusive democratic political structures and processes open and accountable government and inclusive economy[2].

When seen in such a broader context gender equality becomes the essential component of peace discourse. To illustrate, using feminist lens Enloe defines peace as 'women's achievement of control over their lives' and argues that this requires not only absence of armed and gender conflict but also removal of poverty and conditions which give birth to it[3].

What is interesting to note is that despite such significant relation between gender and peace, gender issues remained excluded from dominant peace discourse for a long time. Pankhurast argues that gender issues are not given due space during the conflict settlement talks and post conflict situations. She observes 'where the question of pursuing greater gender equality does arise at the point of settlement, it is uncommon for it to be seen as neither essential nor urgent in peace building'[4]. Emphasizing the need of mainstreaming gender in the fields of conflict resolution and peace studies, Pankhurast argues that bringing gender perspective in the peace studies would enhance the efficiency of peace policies and peace building initiatives[5].

Here, it must be made clear that when feminist scholars emphasize on the relation between peace and women, they want to highlight the multidimensional relation between the two in contrast to conventional discourse on peace where men are seen as 'actors' and 'doers' and women as 'victims' and 'passive recipients'. The feminist researchers argue that women's encounter with wars and conflicts take diverse form and women play diverse roles like 'fighters, community leaders, social organizers, workers, farmers, traders, welfare workers'[6] and so on .

It is interesting to note that women were debarred from peace talks for a long time on the ground that they belong to private and are unexposed to politics and therefore are not fit to be a part of peace talks and negotiations which are only men's domain. But the comprehensive meaning of peace which demands removal of direct, structural and even natural violence has changed the scenario. It would not be wrong to claim that the multidimensional notion of peace has even deconstructed the traditional dichotomy between the public and private. In fact, the recent experiences of post war societies and the role played by women in those societies suggest that women could play larger roles due to their those qualities on the basis of which they were traditionally excluded from peace talks and post-conflict negotiations. To illustrate, women's non-involvement in traditional politics, situatedness in private and their social roles, all these have enabled them in seeing the conflict situations from a different perspective. This can be proved through the experiences of women peace activists. Referring to the emotional strength as the main weapon in the hands of women for peace making, a female activist shared her experience and said that 'both men and women have the potential for peacemaking and the responsibility to build and keep peace. The women, however, seem more creative and effective in waging peace... It is the women's emotional strength to transcend pain and suffering and their predisposition to peace that provided them with greater potentials for peacemaking'[7]. Another peace activist, while sharing her experience during the peace process of the Philippines, argues that women's non-exposure to traditional politics and their different social roles have helped them in seeing the situation from a different perspective. To quote her words: "And here we see that women have played a large role. Perhaps, because of their very lack of exposure to the way traditional politics has been played in this country and the way power has been used, there is in their attitude – and it is not because it is in our genes but because it is in our experience and culture – much less of a kind of 'ego-involvement' which has to be overcome in dealing with the sorts of questions that needs to be done in forging peace for a people that have largely been so divided.... Moreover, women have largely been the survivors and careers of survivors, so this seems to have given them a sustained intensity of wanting to resolve the peace question... Furthermore, through the women, there are possibilities of introducing new paradigms in conflict resolution, because, as I say, we are practised in conflict resolution and conflict transformation in the domestic sphere, that perhaps needs to be played out more to become an input into the way public negotiations take place."[8]

This is really an irony that women's exclusion from politics and power and their confinement to the private which were the tools used by patriarchy to disempower women and to keep them under men's control have enabled women to be better peace-makers and negotiators.

However, there is difference of opinion among the scholars on the question that what do make women more capable peace makers? The diverse views on this question may be divided into two approaches: essentialist view believes that women by nature are peace loving. The female self is pre-dominantly relational and so women have the ability to take and understand perspective of the other. Women are more collaborative then men and so more inclined towards consensus and compromise. This view has been criticized by many for being stereotypical. In contract to this view, the social constructionist view argues that women are more capable peace makers because they are the most vulnerable sufferers during the conflict situations and therefore, resolution of conflicts is in their interest. Further, it argues that the roles assigned to women and their status as mothers and wives and their location at private are the main factors which enable them to play the role of peace makers.

Though, there may be a debate on the matter what does make women better peace makers but on one point there should not be any doubt that women have immense potential to resolve conflicts and establish peace. Therefore, their views must be taken into account on the matter of peace. Acknowledging women's contribution in peace making, U.N. General Secretary, Kofi Annan rightly observes that for generation's women have served as peace educators, both in their families and in their societies. They have been proved instrumental in building bridges rather than wall.' [U.N. Secretary General, Kofi Annan, October, 2000] Similar view has been expressed in the International Alert's code of conduct which states: "We explicitly recognize the particular and distinctive peacemaking roles played by women in conflict afflicted communities. Women and women's organizations are reservoirs of important local capacities which can be used in peace building activities."[9]

On the basis of women's special efforts to establish peace in post-conflict societies even the U.N. has given recognition to women's agency of peace. The U.N. Security Council Resolution 1325 and the Beijing Platform for Action are very significant in this regard. U.N. Security Council Resolution[10] stressed on the need of reaffirming the role of women in prevention and resolution of conflicts and peace building. It emphasized on women's equal participation and full involvement in all efforts for the maintenance and promotion of peace and security. It recognized the urgent need to mainstream a gender perspective into peace making operations. Similar view was expressed very strongly at the Beijing Platform for Action.[11] In the section on 'Women in Armed Conflict emphasize is given on wider participation of women in conflict resolution and peacemaking. It stressed on the need of increasing women's participation in conflict resolution and decision making; promoting non violent forms of conflict resolution and promoting women's contribution to foster a culture of peace.

The above discussion proves that the contemporary discourse on peace is incomplete without feminist perspective. Tickner rightly argues that 'the peace studies curriculum has much to gain by including women's voices. Yet adding women's experiences to the subject matter of our investigation is not enough; feminist perspectives must also expose previously, hiding gender relations in order to demonstrate how gender inequalities can themselves is a source of insecurity.'[12] Thus, there is an urgent need to include women's perspective in peace studies and to move ahead from mere adding women to peace studies.

Notes and References

1. See, J. Galtung, 'Twenty-five Years of Peace Research: Ten Challenges and Responses', *Journal of Peace*, 22(2), 1985 pp. 144-58.
2. See, Donna Pankhurst, The Sex War and other Wars: Towards Feminist Approach to Peace Building, *Development in Practice,* 13:2, 2003, pp. 157-77.
3. See, L. Kelly 'Wars Against Women : Sexual Violence, Sexual Politics and the Militarise State in S. Jocobs, R. Jacobson and Marchbank (eds.), *State of Conflict : Gender, Violence and Resistance,* London, Zed Books, 2000, p. 48.
4. Donna Pankhurast, *op. cit.*, p. 157.
5. *Ibid.*
6. *Ibid.*
7. Quoted in Garcia, E. (ed.), *Pilgrim Voices : Citizens as Peace Makers,* International Alert, 1994, p. 45.
8. *Ibid.*
9. International Alert Gener Campaign, *Women Building Peace: From the Village Council to the Negotiating Table.*, International Alert, London, 1999.
10. U.N. Security Council Resolution 1325 on *'Women, Peace, and Security'*, New York, United Nations, 2002.
11. Beijing Declaration and Platform for Action, Fourth World Conference on Women, United Nations, 1995.
12. J. Ann. Tickner, 'Introducing Feminist Perspective into Peace and World Security Courses', *Women's Studies Quarterly,* Vol. 23, No. ¾, Fall/ Winter 1995, p. 48.

Peace—A Need of the Hour

15

SANGEETA

Today in the world, there are many walls among humans that are a cause of hatred and disharmony. All the barriers are man-made. No wall or barrier has been created by God. We may have progressed in the fields of science and technology, but we are still backward when it comes to living a righteous life. Humans bow in front of the scriptures and visit holy places, but fail to live up to the words and messages of the Saints and Seers mentioned in those holy books. This is ignorance. All of us irrespective of our nationalities, languages, cultures are one. Saints and sages have defined the same thought in many words. But man remains oblivious and careless to adopt this essence in his life which is resulting into strife and war all across.

The World has become a place of fear, sorrow, disharmony and pain. It is because of absence of love and harmony. People are divided on the basis of Nationality, creed and religion. They are not ready to believe that God is One, that's why in the name of God Almighty, they are hating each other..... then Where is a feeling of Oneness? Where is Peace??..... unless we have the realization of single entity of God, we cannot be one. Harmony makes small things grow and lack of it makes great things decay. Thus, decay process is going on because there is no harmony. We have to ponder upon these facts and we have to evaluate ourselves, our thought process and our feelings.

Apparently, Gandhi seemed to favour conflict by inspiring the oppressed of the world, for their emanicipation but he never made conflict as the law of society as Karl Marx did. He always gave the methodolgy of non-violent conflict resolution (elimination of conflict). The nature and techniques of his struggles both in the procedures and achievements, are such that they gradually remove the tension, conflicts and opposition and ultimately pave the way for a harmonious society and world order. In International politics, war is the most important form of conflict which was opposed by Mahatma Gandhi by tooth and nail. He used to go into the detail of the problem of war and tried to provide a moral alternative to abolish it. So his method of non-violence is actually a method of conflict resolution.[1]

Pyarelal, a close associate of Mahatma Gandhi in his article, "Gandhian analysis of the causes of international tensions and war" has summarized the essential conditions of the New World Order and suggested some measures to fulfill these conditions on Gandhian lines.[2] In his view, equality and independence of all nations, "Swadeshi as a fulcrum of universalism" removal of the causes of international tensions, adoption of Trusteeship as a means for the removal of inequalities and Satyagraha for the removal of social injustice and a ceaseless determined struggle against the passions of selfishness, lust and greed are some of the important conditions of the New World, with which, most of the conflicts will not take place in international world.

Gandhi is one of the very relevant precursors of conflict-resolution movement with his comprehensible philosophy of peace based on the psychology of human nature, awareness of social realities and knowledge of economic and political systems and situations. As long as there is violence which threatens the very future of the human race, the relevance of Gandhiji would continue. He will remain relevant till the changes of total annihilation of the human race are removed. Peace is the relationship between people and people. Peace begins with the harmony between individuals. Gandhi lived and worked for the establishment of such relationship among individuals and groups. His is a unique contribution to peace in the modern world context. Gandhi's style of life and techniques he propounded deserved to be studied and applied so that the world may be a safe place to live in.

In a human society conflicts will always be there between individuals, between groups, between nations because of differences of opinion, clash of interest, establishment of superiority and various other factors. Economic depriviation and social subjugation are the basic causes of conflicts in human society. It is a continuous trend of torturing the weak by more powerful individuals or groups, exploitation of the poor by rich and landed people, hatred of upper class people on the lower caste people, neglect of illiterate people by the educated people, socially over-powering women by men and such other injustices. These types of injustices are the constant cause of discontent in the society which give rise to conflicts. The main concern is that these problems are not being solved but suppressed. With the progress in civilization and development of humanistic attitude, people are now gradually getting more and more concerned with Human Rights that demand social justice for all sections of the society.

The need of ours is to proclaim again and again the significance of Gandhian methods to solve crucial problems of conflicts and violence. To prevent structural violence, Gandhi proposed the theories with ideals of Satyagraha, Sarvodaya, Swaraj, Buniyadi Talim, Decentralization of Power, and wealth, Trusteeship, Social Harmony and Communal unity, Economic equality, Sarva Dharma Sambhava, Democracy of Enlightened Majority, etc.

The invention of devastating deadly weapons and armament race, wrongly conceived as the symbol of power and security, bring suspicion in the mind of every nation and create psychological tension in global level. War can never be a method of Conflict resolution and therefore Gandhi proposed and adopted "Satyagraha" as a moral equivalent to war and conflict based on the principles of non-violence. It aims at winning over an opponent by love and gentle persuading and by arousing in him a sense of justice rather than forcing him to surrender out of fear. Satyagrahi aims at the conversion of the opponent's heart by making him aware of his ill-will or inhuman behaviour through self-suffering. The method of Satyagraha is purely moral and humanistic as it involoves faith in the inherent goodness and good sense of the opponent coupled with goodwill towards him and readiness to come to an understanding and compromise. Infact Satyagraha aims at settlement of issue or issues with the opponent without causing him even psychological injury but it implies soul-force, courage and determination.

Gandhi is known for holding truth. Truth is the pole star of his life and philosophy. To Gandhi, truth is the sovereign principle which includes numerous principles and his whole life is experiment with the truth. Note the title of his autobiography styled as "The Story of My Experiments with Truth".[3] According to Gandhi the Truth alone can resolve conflict and peace can occur only in truthful environment. Fear, anger, hatred, deceit and cowardice lead to conflict and peace doesnot have a place in such an environment. Being truthful is more important than peaceful. Non-violence is a logical corollary to the principle of truth to him. To Gandhi "ahimsa is the means, truth is the end".[4] He had a living and unshakeable faith that truth can be realized only by means of ahimsa. When it was taunted that his non-violence is a policy of helpless persons, then he used to say,"Non-violence is not a cover for cowardice but it is the supreme virtue of the brave".[5] It doesnot mean meek submission to the will of tyrant.[6]

In Gandhian philosophy, Means and Ends are closely interwined like the two sides of a coin. Nevertheless, ahimsa is the means; truth is the end. Means to be means must always be within our reach, and so ahimsa is our supreme duty. If we take care of the means, we are bound to reach the end sooner or later. As a matter of fact, Gandhi's prescription of moral means for the settlement of internal disputes is extended to the settlement of international disputes as well.

The most fundamental principle of Gandhi's philosophy of peace is "Ahimsa" or non-violence which is law of love, life and creation as opposed to violence or Himsa, the cause of hatred, death and destruction. Negatively it is absence of mental intention of injuring, harming, disturbing and agonising opponent, and Positively it is good will towards all human beings. As a peaceful technique to resist injustice, it includes a concrete programme and leads to self-suffering and sacrifice. For Gandhi "Fasting unto death" is the last step to oppose injustice.

While appreciating the role of non-violence in a larger context, Albert Einstein commented "..... in our age of moral decay Gandhi was the only statesman who represented that higher conception of human relations in the political sphere to which we must aspire with all our power. We must learn the difficult lesson that the future of mankind will be tolerable only when our course in world affairs as well in other matters is based on justice and law, rather than on the threat of naked power....".[7]

Similar kind of thoughts have also been echoed by N. Radhakrishnan about Gandhi when he says that India failed to project Gandhi who offerred healthy vision of life based on self-respect, self-help, non-exploitation, non-violence, and transcendental eco-friendly-in short, a definite alternative to the manipulative, violent, and exploitative world order.[8]

Not much research has been conducted on this very issue till the middle of this century. Gandhi has been the shining example of the twentieth century who employed his peaceful methods for bringing about a larger peace. In 1968 Willy Brandt, while delievering his speech at UNESCO Conference highlighted the peaceful co-existence as the spirit of solidarity. He added to his speech that peace is not merely the absence of war and violence in the human society. We must commit to our memory that the peace demands freedom from oppression from hunger and from ignorance. People can flourish and develop their capacities freely and responsibly to their fullest contexts only under these conditions.[9]

Gandhi also suggested a technique of "Sarva Dharma Sambhav" in order to prevent conflicts caused by religious bigotry. According to him all religions are true and man cannot live without religion so he recommends attitude of respect and tolerance towards all religions. Since the scientific and technological researches aimed at material comforts ruining human sensitivity and sentiments i.e. human feelings and relations, so scientists and technocrats must be reminded of their moral obligation to choose peaceful means and so to perform their first and prior duty towards humanity. They should not invent biological, chemical, nuclear, laser and other kinds of sophisticated weapons, which verifies the assumption that science and technology one frequently used as instruments of exploitation, domination and destruction rather than as means in the service of mankind and peace.

Total disarmament is the need of an hour but it cannot take place until and unless the hearts and minds of persons who manufacture, sale and purchase weapons are changed. Public pressure could play an important role. Gandhi believed that disarmament was possible only through " the matchless weapon of non-violence," and it was his hope that India will prove herself worthy of being the first nation in the world to give lead to other nations in this regard. He wanted the great powers lead the rest by disarming themselves: they should give up ambitions and exploitation and revise their mode of life. Thus, according to Gandhi, disarmament cannot crystallise, unless the nations of the world cease to exploit one another. Non-violence according to him, excludes war and ushers in peace. He to stand for non-violence and non-exploitative social order which alone can ensure just and enduring peace. It may be argued that the Gandhian declarations on peace bristle with some practical difficulties. But Gandhi would ask that- if an individual could practice non-violence why whole nations could not do so? He believed that one must make a beginning and the rest would follow. The Gandhian concept of world peace should be viewed within the general framework of his philosophy of ahimsa.

"Peace will never come until the great powers courageously decide to disarm themselves. Exploitation and domination of one nation over another can have no place in a world striving to put amend to all wars. In such a world only the militarily weaker nations will be free from the fear of intimidation or exploitation. I have no doubt that unless big nations shed their desire of exploitation and the spirit of which war is the natural expression and atom bomb an inevitable consequence, there is no hope for peace in the world."[10]

The world, has become a small family as a result of the extraordinary growth of Science and Technology, but at the same time it has added new dimensions not to violence and destruction. The question facing the humanity today is not to choose between violence and non-violence but to choose between destruction and survival. Humanity has failed to learn lessons from history. The most tragic part of this episode is while we are quick to discern disaster, we do precious little to cry a halt to it. The choice before humanity today is co-existence or co-extinction. Gandhiji is of the firm opinion that war can never end wars. Violence breeds only violence but can never end violence. War is destructive whereas peace is constructive. They are two opposite processes. Further violence being, being destructive, is a negative process, whereas peace, being constructive, is a positive process. Peace is a positive force of cementing people. War which is a destroying and divisive force can never contribute to the establishment of peace. Hence, the search for peace should be in the way of non-violence alone.

According to Rev. Martin Luther King: "the choice before mankind is between non-violence and non-existence". Gandhi ji was often associated with unilateral disarmament. As a messiah of peace and non-violence, he repeatedly asserted the supremacy of moral force over physical force. Gandhi ji has in his armoury weapons to promote world peace even in this nuclear age.

Some nations want to establish supremacy over the other nations. They derive to create and perpetuate inequalities for this purpose a vicious circle of self aggrandisement and inequality can be broken only by an international law by which all nations are treated as equal and then it will go a long way to establish peace in the world.

The United Nations is upholding a certain point of co-existence between the big powers through its six principle organs like the General Assembly, the Security Council. The Economic and Social Council, the trusteeship Council, the Secretariat and the International Court of Justice. Together they are able to deal with all types of international problems- economic, social and developed areas, disputes between nations, aggression[11] and breaches of peace. The facilities which they offer can be used for conference for the negotiation programmes of action, for the application of sanctions against an aggressor for the settlement of international controversies, for research, for investigation, for publicity and for purpose of international administration.

It is true that some of the principles underlying the United Nation can be cited as in harmony with those of Gandhi's non-violent social order. Thus Secretary General U.Thant on the occasion of the Gandhian centenary observed that," many of the ideals of Mahatma Gandhi are in line with the principle and purposes of the Charter of the United Nations. For instance, the Charter calls upon us to refrain from the threat or use of force in article 2, paras 3 and 4 and Article 33 states that in international disputes the parties shall first of all seek a solution by Negotiations inquiry, Mediation, Conciliation, Arbitration, Judicial settlement resort to regional agencies or arrangements or other peaceful means of their own choice. But in modern war although the United Nations can be regarded as means to international order through conflict control, the theory nonetheless makes allowance for violence as a last resort after availing all the peaceful non-violent norms. In Post Gandhian violent era there is a mood of restlessness and a desire for change. But peace and security among nations can be achieved only through the elimination of all concepts of violence from the minds of men for which the United Nations as yet has not taken any step. Moreover, the United Nations can be effective in restraining the parties to the dispute from using violence for the resolution of their conflicts only when there is n agreement among the great powers in doing so. If the conflict in the region.serves the purpose of the great powers United Nations become more or less ineffective. It is mostly reduced to a debating society. That accounts for several wars and mini wars or civil wars which are going on in the Third World Countries.[12]

Alliance means the state of union or combination for a common object. They are one of the primary means by which states seek the cooperation of other states in order to enhance their power to protect and advance their interests. An alliance is, therefore, a formal agreement between two or more than two nations to collaborate among themselves on national security issues. Since the alliances are reciprocal and formal agreements, they increase the obligation of signatories to carry out specified commitment and cooperation. The alliances may be defensive or offensive. A defensive alliance pre-supposes only a common interest in opposing threats from specific states or groups outside the alliance and doesnot necessarily or usually entail provisions for setting disputes among its members. An offensive alliance aims at forcibly changing the international *status-quo* territorially or otherwise to increase the assets of its members. But alliances cannot be the save guarantee for permanent peace. For, any alliance can be upset by a new development in world power politics.

Deterrence in the most general sense is the dissuasion of one adversary by another from undertaking hostile military action by convincing him that such an action would be unsuccessful or too costly since it would incur military counteraction. In simple terms, if deterrence, is used simply to prevent an enemy initiating against an action of which one is afraid, its effect is defensive if on the other hand it is used to prevent the enemy resisting some action which one proposes to take oneself, deterrence is offensive. This offensive or defensive action may be either direct or indirect depending upon its use either between two opponents or for the benefit of a third party.

Disarmament means an action of disarming, to deprive of means of attack or to divest of hostility etc. in a broad sense, it implies the reduction or limitation of the size, equipment, armament and armed forces. The problem of controlling the arms race has attracted the attention of the world public for more than a century. At the end of the nineteenth century when Europe was overburdened by arms growth, Fredrich Engels recognized that there was an alternative to a devastating war on a scale the world had not seen before: this was 'Disarmament' which is possibly also a guarantee of peace. In every way efforts are being made to distinguish disarmament among various possible forms. In the world of today where armaments if not used as a means of influencing the relation between communities can be covered under the terminology of General and Complete Disarmament (GCD). The other way is through conventions when all states would not agree to abolish armaments altogether. But would freeze them through mutually agreed levels. The form 'Arms Control' will mean adopting of limited measures in some countries or involving only particular weapons. This last form is also prevalent today.

The continued arms race, the accumulation of weapons of mass destruction and the accelerated work on new types of such weapons have led to unprecedented activities by men of all countries for arms control or convention. Several voluntary peace associations in the world are carrying on propaganda for nuclear disarmament—Campaign for Nuclear Disarmament (CND), European Nuclear Disarmament (END) and 'Ban the Bomb Movement' are building up public opinion against the manufacture of nuclear armaments. As a result, moves for disarmament agreement have been going on, for the enhancement of peace in the modern world.

However, the majority hindrance to disarmament today is the imperialistic designs of the major power of the world and their plans to exploit the less powerful countries of the world. The nation have to find escape from the impending doom for which unconditional acceptance of non-violent method is required, which who involves unilateral disarmament. According to Gandhi it would be a miracle if the great powers accepted his ideas, but he also added that miracles have happened before and may happen again perhaps, with the power shown by him in non-violence and peace.

There are three well-known approaches to the question of the elimination of war. One is through peace conferences, the other through universal disarmament, and the third through the establishment of a world government or a world organisation for peaceful settlement of disputes between nations and restoration of peace when a breach of it occurs. Experience has shown that the peace of the world has often been broken while peace conferences were actually being held, and disarmament conferences often provide to armament manufacturers a happy hunting ground where they find their best customers for military hardware. We have today a world organisation that depends, by and large, on the sanction of force to back its decisions. Being veto-ridden, it cannot apply that sanction to problems over which the two major power blocs differ, and hence it has itself become an arena of conflict between the power blocs.

So long as there is no sanction other than force for the settlement of disputes, all attempts to ensure the peace of the world by negotiation or by the abolition or limiting of armaments, whether nuclear or conventional are bound to end. A world organisation backed by a moral or non-violent sanction can guarantee international peace. It is here that Gandhi's contribution to the solution of the problem comes to our rescue.

We all wish to eradicate tensions whether national or international. Everybody wants peace. But there may be something worse than a breach of peace, namely, perpetuation of the peace of the grave. Gandhi had no use for peace that served to maintain the *status quo*, by the perpetuation of existing inequalities and injustice; he wanted peace that resulted from the realisation of justice and ensure equality and independence of all. But the nature of independence is bound to "correspond to the extent of non-violence assimilated by the nations concerned". Gandhi, therefore, further insisted that the participating units in the world organisation for peace should have banished violence from their internal polity. Wars do not originate at the battle fronts. Nor does peace return automatically when actual fight ceases. The intervals between wars serve but too often as incubating periods for the next war. The roots of war lie deep in causes that are endemic in our society. International tensions are often a projection of intranational tensions- socio-economic tensions within the nations. To ensure international peace, however, we have to eradicate these internal tensions.

The most important cause of tension, both international and intranational, according to Gandhi, is exploitation. Personal ambition and ideological fanaticism are subsidiary to it. Ideological fanaticism and nationalism are used as a mask as well as an excitement to mislead and work up the popular mind. Essentially, war is resorted to by the so-called advanced countries for the political control of undeveloped and under-developed countries in order to secure markets for their surplus products and a source of cheap raw material and labour for their industry. The same end, however, can be secured at much less cost and without attracting world attention by financial and economic control. Today the highly industrialised states—whether capitalist, socialist or communist— are vying with one another in extending their industrial domain. There can be no peace in the world so long as this continues.

A country must be at peace with itself before it can be with its neighbours. There must be harmony among various regions and classes. To have international peace, therefore, said Gandhi, the economy of the participating units must "be free from exploitation in every shape and form—exploitation by the rich of the poor, of the masses by the classes, of the village by the town and of the weaker or so-called undeveloped races by the stronger and the more advanced ones". Interdependence there must be, but it should be on the basis of mutual benefit which is the *sine qua non* of real cooperation. If my gain spells another's loss then it will not make for peace. But if my gain means my neighbour's gain also and the gain of all, it will make for a real and lasting peace.

The question of world peace thus ultimately resolves itself into one of achieving a conquest of self. The coercive machinery of the state becomes a necessity for the preservation of society, when our love of self gets the better of our love of others. Exercise of coercion creates in those who exercise it the habit of coercion and in course of time the state itself, instead of serving as a means of preventing coercion, becomes an instrument of coercion—first of the people who established it and then of the neighbouring people. The only way of escape from this vicious circle is, in the words of Gandhi, to submit ourselves to "disciplined rule from within".

Gandhi accordingly in his Indian Home Rule defined Swaraj or self-rule as "rule over self". "The root meaning of Swaraj", he observed, "is self-rule or disciplined rule from within; the outward freedom....that we shall attain will therefore only be in exact proportion to the inward freedom to which we may have grown at a given moment". It is only in such freedom that the ideal of international peace and of a warless world can be realized.

For countering aggression and preservation of international peace, the necessary conditions laid down by Gandhi are:

1. Equality and independence of all nations, big and small.
2. To foster nationalism as a means and stepping stone to internationalism; and Swadeshi as a fulcrum of universalism.
3. Removal of the causes of intranational tensions of which international tensions are very often a projection. Adoption of 'trusteeship' as a means for the removal of inequalities and of Satyagraha for the removal of social injustice.
4. A ceaseless determined struggle against the passions of selfishness, lust and greed within us of which violence and aggression are compounded, and inculcation of the same in the people at large. In other words, to progressively substitute for outer discipline, self-discipline or "disciplined rule from within".

To this end he recommended:

a) Attainment of self-sufficiency so far as possible in respect of all vital needs for existence at regional as well as national level.
b) Eradication of all exploitation or domination—by the rich of the poor, of the masses by the classes, of the village by the town, and of the weaker or so-called undeveloped races by the stronger and the more advanced ones.
c) Adoption of decentralised economy in the true sense of the word and a system of regional autonomy on the widest scale, subject to the safeguarding of certain fundamental rights for all.
d) Adoption of a way of life and culture based on the principles of self-discipline, self-restraint, 'bread labour' and creative satisfaction, as opposed to the doctrine that regards all labour as the "curse of Adam" and makes a God of self-indulgence, and unrestrained consumerism, and of a social and economic system conducive and contributory to it.[13]

Gandhiji has often been described as an apostle of peace. He strove and died for peace. He advocated "peace—but not any price" for his philosophy was a philosophy of commitment. His philosophy of peace is to be differentiated from the conservative plea for peace at any cost. He saw peace as integrally related to justice. Peace is not mere cessation of hostilities. He did not share the diplomatic view of peace. Peace for him meant a positive state of affairs, the pre-condition being freedom from exploitation. In his opinion, only non-violent and just peace could ensure lasting peace.

To abolish war, we must get rid of our anger, hate, passion, pride, cupidity, fear, egotism and inordinate ambition and lust for power. We must so reorganise our economic structure as to eliminate exploitation of man by man and of one people by another. There should surely be increase in production, but it must be accompanied by increase in live and sympathy as well. People must also be made to realise that peace has an independent value and should be sought after its own sake.

The problem arises as to how man can realise peace. According to Toynbee, "The source of peace and war is the interior of life of each individual human spirit". We should not forget that man is the source the centre and purpose of all life. Peace begins in our own hearts. The universality of spirit lies not in knowing much, but in loving extensively. Peace is really the reflection of heaven upon earth. In the Hebrew language, the word "shalom" means peace with justice. It means inner security and external excess. He will be a man of peace who has in him the combination of both. Arnold Toynbee espousing the cause of peace observed: "when the pursuit of peace is whole-hearted, it covers every aspect of human affairs.

To establish peace, the following aspects may be considered:

1. A conviction of the fundamental unity of the human family and the equality and dignity of all human beings.
2. A sense of sacredness of the individual person and his concience.
3. A sense of the value of human community.
4. A realisation that might is not right, that human power is not self-sufficient and absolute.
5. A belief that love, compassion, selfishness and the force of inner truthfulness and of the spirit have ultimately greater power than hate, enmity and self-interest.
6. A sense of obligation to stand on the side of the poor and the oppressed as against the rich and the oppressed.
7. A profound hope that good will finally prevail.

8. Man's spiritual and moral maturity must grow proportionately to his technical skill and power. It can be done if science and religion get together and work together in a harmonious relationship.
9. Commitment to violence cannot guarantee security, but universal commitment to practical non-violent alternatives can make us personally nationally and globally much more secure.
10. "Education for Peace" must be a subject for bringing forth creative human potential in the family, work, place and community.
11. No scheme of global peace can prove lasting unless it is linked to the creation of a new equitable world economic order. There can be no lasting world peace unless the basic factors of exploitation and hegemony are removed.
12. The greatest need today more than ever before is to educate the people and their governments to have a greater understanding and awareness of the problems created by armaments race and of the need for disarmament.[14]

Feeling of oneness should be the common ground and operative principle of all our actions. We have to live together, we can't banish anyone and tell them to go away from this planet. We have to keep this in mind in the common factor of being children of the same ONE GOD so that we can love all as our brothers and sisters, bringing the thought of Oneness to life.

Peace does not imply any kind of cowardice to him. Peace of weak was not accepted to him. According to Gandhi ji a strong willed and able to protect oneself-person can achieve and establish peace. Gandhiji believed that cowardice as worse than violence. " I do believe that, where there is only a choice between cowardice and violence, I would advice violence". At other place Gandhiji opined " I would rather have India resort to arms in order to defend her honour than that she would in a cowardly manner become or remain a helpless witness to her own dishonour".[15] Thus Gandhiji's appeal for non-violent methods to establish peace never included peace of cowards. Self-prestige, honour was supreme to him.

Gandhi ji sought to prepare us for life in a disarmed world. We must pull ourselves of the world of strive and hatred and be prepared to work unitedly with a sense of harmony and peace. Peace is not the absence of conflict but the ability to cope with it. It was in this spirit that Gandhi ji worked and prayed towards the realisation of peace among men. The Gandhian message posses demands on man for the cultivation of good will, love and non-violence, because man, in Gandhian view, is supposedly capable of responding. Man must revaluate himself, subdue his flesh to soul, limit his wants, and teach himself self-effort, sacrifice and non-violence. On the basis of this transformation the world would know genuine peace that would apply equally well to inter-personal affairs as well as to international ones. While fundamental assumptions cannot be proved or disproved and perfection is impossible, still perfectability is always possible.

It is very shocking to note that no serious and sustained consideration is given to human search for peace or peace studies in academic institution and syllabi, while ours is a world of nuclear giants and moral infants. Each and every citizen of the world must be educated to escape conflict, as ultimately person himself is the insurmountable barrier in conflict resolution. Awareness and awakening of creative qualities must be a part of education policy and curriculum. Instead of over-emphasising destructive instincts, we must try to make a person cultured by encouraging to cultivate constructive aspects of his personality, because constructive aspect is related to human values and virtues as well as their incorporation in cognitive, conative and affective dimension of our personality.

Gandhi's approach is ethical, as he believes that moral degeneration is the root cause of all evils including conflicts, so he recommends acquistion of moral value such as truthfulness, non-violence or love, self-control, forgiveness, non-enmity or friendliness, compassion, mercy, etc. Infact, values are the best equipments discovered by human being to escape various types of conflict. Gandhi appreciates moral solution, which is inexpensive and single person can initiate and undertake the task of conflict resolution by attracting worldwide attention. Public awareness of those values which are conducive to peace buliding must be evoked through exhibition, education, public lectures, dialogues and mass communication- T.V., Radio, Newspapers, etc.

Only slogan for 'peace' cannot change the society. We need to work for it by cultivating humanistic education by covering various aspects responsible for creating social discontents giving rise to conflicts and emphasizing on maintaining peace in conflict resolution, and thus to create a society worth living as Gandhi visioned and worked for. Gandhi has been the champion not only of political democracy but also of economic and spiritual democracy as he committed to the Vedantic view of unity in multiplicity and was a supporter of economic equality.

May the life and teachings of Mahatma Gandhi be a beacon of hope and courage to all of us. The teachings of Mahatma will continue to be relevant till humanism, betterment of the human condition, world peace, and conflict of resolution by non-violence continues to be relevant and urgently desirable. Let us catch the spirit of Gandhiji's teaching and help to create the kind of society that the Mahatma envisaged. Gandhiji called upon humanity to strengthen its conscience, steel its will, and be ready for the highest sacrifice for establishing the truth of human equality, dignity, fraternity and freedom.

Notes and References

1. The New Webster Encyclopaedia Dictionary of the English language (Consolidated Book Publisher, Chicago), p. 177.
2. Walter, L. Walace, *Sociological Theory* (Heine ann., London), 1969; p. 214.
3. Mahatma,Gandhi, *The Story of My Experiment With Truth.*
4. *CWMG*, September 21, 1934, Vol. xix, p. 43.
5. *Young India*, 12-8-26.
6. *Ibid.*, 11-8-20.
7. Einstein, Albert, "*On Peace and Gandhi*", in Richard B. Gregg, Profiles in Gandhi, p. 100.
8. Radhakrishnan, N.: *The Quest for Tolerance and Survival.*
9. Brandt, Willy, "Peaceful Co-existence in the spirit of solidarity", speech at UNESCO Conference held on 6 November 1968.
10. *Journal of Gandhian Studies,* Edited by Prof. J.S. Mathur, Institute of Gandhian Thought and Peace Studies, University of Allahabad, p. 109.
11. Sydney D. Bailey, *The United Nations* (Pall Mali Press, London, 1963), p. 53.
12. *India News,* 5 October 1968, Quoted in Francis Paraktil, *India and United Nations Peace Keeping Operations* (Delhi: S. Chand & Co. Pvt. Ltd., 1975), p. 30.
13. Misra, K.P., Gangal S.C., *Gandhi and the Contemporary World- Studies in Peace and War*, (Chanakya Publications, Delhi, 1981), p. 109.
14. Maharajan, M., *Mahatma Gandhi and The New Millennium,* (Discovery Publishing House, New Delhi, 2001), p. 38.
15. Gandhi, M.K., Non-violence in Peace and War.

India's Regional Security

A Foreign Policy Priority

16

VIJAY CHAUHAN

India as a Nation-State has always remained concerned about its security. As security is always contextual, and situational, can only be defined and ensured keeping in view time and space. Its keeps on changing with the change of context. In this research exercise, modest attempt is made to look at India's regional security concerns. The first section of this paper researcher define the concept of 'National Security'. This is followed by explanation of India's regional security challenges. Throughout this paper, the effort has been to examine India's regional security concerns in the long run and in broader perspective.

The political, economic and social landscape in India's immediate neighbourhood has changed significantly since the end of the Cold War.[1] One of the most striking things about the larger Asian strategic landscape is the arc of failing or troubled states around India. This harsh geographical reality is India's most-glaring weaknesses—one that weighs it down regionally. Its neighbourhood is so chronically troubled that India confronts what can be called a tyranny of geography. As a result, it faces serious external threats from virtually all directions. It is locked in an arc of failing or authoritarian states that seek, in different ways, to undermine its secular, multiethnic, pluralistic character. In order to grasp the relative weight of today's regional security challenge, traditional concept of national security is being broadened gradually to include human security concerns.[2] This paper discuss India's various regional security challenges relevant to today, and conclude by re-examine the historical trend to determine if India is likely to manage these challenges effectively, as it negotiate its rise to great power status in the foreign policy sphere.

NATIONAL SECURITY DEFINED

National Security is a key concept for those who engage in analysis of foreign policy. This is equally true for practitioner, who is engaged in the process of formulating their respective state's foreign policy. National security means different things to different people, and there is no universally agreed understanding of what the term signifies. Although the traditional meaning of national security is most often associated with the notion of protecting, and ultimately securing, the physical survival of the notion-state from external threats in the form of a military attack, this certainly does not exhaust all of the possible meanings. The ambiguity surrounding the concept of national security stems from a number of factors. First, the term 'security', like that of other concepts such as power, is extremely broad and can be viewed from a variety of cometing perspectives. Writings in 1983, *Barry Buzun*, in his highly acclaimed book *People, State, and Fear*, reconfirmed wolfers' point by arguing that security remained an undevelopment concept (Buzan). A key question, therefore, is what do we really mean by security? Is security limited to military concerns or should other issues such as health, the economy, and the environment be included as 'security issues'? unfortunately the answer to this question depends on how one answer the related question of what or who is the proper referent of the object of security. Who, or what, are we attempting to secure? Depends on your perspective, there are a number of possible referent obects: individuals, families, nation state, regions, the society of state and even the globe. Although the traditional perspective holds that the referent objects of security is the nation-state, there are those who endorse the concept of human security, pointing instead to the possibility of individual being the referent object of security. If we take seriously the idea that the aim of national security is to secure individuals, a diverse range of issues and concerns enters the framework of analysis. India as a nation-state has always remained concerned about its security. It faces numerous contemporary security challenges, mostly regional. India still grapples with a number of important security and political challenge at home, in its region, and globally. On the domestic front, while opening the political space to new social groups has deepened democracy in India, it has also led to serve political fragmentation and often creates obstacle to effective policymaking. India's region is fraught with security threats arising out of unstable, often weak states such as Pakistan, Sri Lanka, Nepal, Bangladesh, Myanmar and Afghanistan, a near-neighbour in which India is much invested.[3]

REGIONAL SECURITY CHALLENGES

By some measures, six of India's neighbours ranked in the top twenty-five dysfunctional state in the world as calculated by the Failed States Index of the fund for peace.[4] India is uniquely positioned to be a driver of interstate cooperation in South Asia, which is "predominantly Indocentric region' because in term of religion or culture or both. 'India has something in common with [each of] its immediate neighbours but the neighbouring states of India do not share similarities of such magnitude or depth among themselves'.[5] Yet India is unable to bring about such cooperation, and despite the great strides it has made in economic growth over the last two decades, it remain mired the security dilemmas in its own region. As Vikram Sood suggest, 'Globally, India is being recognized as a rising economic power but not in the region where economic development has become hostage to security issue.[6] Another scholar describes India's regional status as one of 'contested dominance', with India dominant because it lacks a convincing regional rival, but not enjoying supremacy because 'its lacks a convincing regional rival, but not enjoying supremacy because 'its dominance in the region is not accepted and acknowledge by its neighbours'.[7] As a result, India faces two main regional challenges. The first is a set what might otherwise be classified as domestic law-and-order problems were it not for the involvement of India's neighbours. Challenges of sub-national ethnic identity, secessionist movements and insurgencies, the creation of new ethnic communities due to migration, and religious conflict within India fall under his heading. The second relates to bilateral disputes between India and its neighbour over resources, particularly land and water. Territorial disputes (prominently, Kashmir and Siachen with Pakistan and Arunachal resources, which have become more frequent and more consequential over the decades since India's independence, and other security challenges emanating directly from India's neighbours, conform to this category.[8]

SUB-NATIONAL ETHNIC MOVEMENTS

Indian populations in border region tend to share common ethnic bonds with populations in adjacent countries. This is true of Tamils and Sri Lanka, Muslims in Kashmir, Punjabis, Indian populations bordering the Tarai region of Nepal and even Malayalis and their ties to Gulf countries. By corollary, Hindu minorities in Bangladesh and Pakistan share affinities with co-religionists across the border in India. Trafficking of all sorts across mostly pretty open borders (Pakistan's being the exception) presents particular challenges in these circumstances. The border territorial division of ethnic groups within India and the strength of regional ethnic identities ensure that Indian policy towards the countries in question is often attentive to the preference of domestic actors in these regions, as with Sri Lanka, where, at one time, the Indian government acquiesced in the brutal armed tactics of the Liberation Tiger of Tamil Eelam (LTTE).[9] Similarly, there is 'widespread sympathy' in Indian border regions for the Madhesi campaign for autonomy in the tarai region of Nepal and moat [Indian] politicians and bureaucrats do not hesitate to express moral support for it.[10]

SECESSIONIST MOVEMENTS AND INSURGENCES

Due to India's vast size and heterogeneous society and policy, conflicts have proliferated between sub-national regions and the central government. Scholars have attributed this to the failure of the Indian state to ensure equitable development for large swathes of society. This, they argue, has resulted in the discrediting of state-sponsored nationalism and, *inter alia,* the rise of movements aimed at establishment separate sovereign status from the union.[11] The history of modern India is replete with such movements, many of which are still in progress. Movements in border area are particularly problematic because they become flashpoint with neighbouring countries, mainly for two reasons. First, secessionist movements, especially armed movements, are likely to use the territories of adjacent countries (e.g. Myanmar, Bhutan, Pakistan, Nepal, China, and Bangldesh) to stage their attack on the Indian state, making it harder to neutralize the insurgents. Second, they allow neighbours countries with an interest in destabilizing India to interfere in its internal affairs in an adverse manner. (This would apply, in the minds of most Indians, mainly to Pakistan). These are the consideration that have influenced India's policy towards Pakistan in the case of the Khalistan and Kashmir secessionist movements.[12] But they are also relevant to Burma, Bhutan, China, and Bangladesh in the case of Multiple movements in the northeast.[13] And, while somewhat different, they would also apply to Nepal in the case of the widespread Indian naxalite movements (although not strict a secessionist movement, but vigorously anti state nonetheless).

NEW ETHNIC GROUPS

The cross border movements of large populations from neighbours countries into India over extended periods of time results in the creation of new ethnic groups in the border (and other) region of India, thus complicating Indian policy towards the originating countries. Two examples stand out–the migration of Tibetans escaping Chinese persecution and the steady inflows of immigrants (legal or illegal) from Bangladesh into West Bengal and the north-eastern regions of India (many of them subsequently moving well beyond these regions). These developments have impacted on India's relations with China and Bangladesh respectively. In the case of China, India has walked a tightrope between official recognition of Tibet as an integral part of China and granting asylum to the Dalai Lama and his followers on Indian territory. Tibetan migrants have integrated relatively well into Indian Society, finding geographic and economic niches that do not conflict with local arrangements to a great extent. By contrast, the domestic response to Bangladesh immigrants has been much less forgiving, possibly due to their purely economic motivation for migration. The reaction has been violent in Assam, where riots against migrant Bengalis date back to the 1960s and 1970s. This has produced a negative impact on Indo-Bangladesh relations, which are further complicated by a host of others bilateral issues.[14]

BILATERAL ISSUES : PAKISTAN

Coping with the threats emanating from Pakistan is likely to be the most important security challenge for India in the coming years. Over two and a half decades, successive governments in Delhi, of very different political hues, have sought to normalize relations with Pakistan but without much success. At the root of India's difficulty with Pakistan have been the changing regional balance of power and Rawalpindi's new freedom to promote a low-intensity conflict against Delhi. The shift of the regional balance of power in favour of India following the breakup of Pakistan in 1971 was successfully reversed by Rawalpindi's acquisition of a nuclear deterrent by the late 1980s. Having neutralized India's conventional military superiority, the Pakistan Army has had the impunity to support anti-India terror groups that mounted frequent spectacular attacks in India. But Delhi's efforts to negotiate new *modus vivendi* with Islamabad have been stymied by the multiple centers of power in Pakistan and Rawalpindi's reluctance to end its support to anti-India terror groups. Despite these difficulties, India has traversed some distance with Pakistan over the last few years. After a series of military crises from the late 1980s to early 2000s, India worked out a negotiating framework with Pakistan that involved three elements: India's willingness to negotiate on Kashmir, Pakistan's commitment to end cross-border terrorism, and the expansion of confidence building measures. As a result there were periods of relative lull in the intensity of cross-border terrorism, back channel negotiations on Kashmir, and the institution of a range of military, political and economic CBMs. This framework, however, appeared to be breaking down in 2013 amidst the frequent violation of a decade-long ceasefire in Kashmir, Islamabad's reluctance to bring the plotters of the 26/11 attack on Mumbai to justice, and its inability to implement the trade normalization agreement.[15]

BILATERAL ISSUES : CHINA

Increasingly, China is more worrying for India than is Pakistan, whatever the provocation launched against India from within the latter's territory. While India has experienced significant economic success over the past twenty years, China initiated its economic reforms well before India did, and has consistently outstripped India's impressive growth by 2-3 per cent each year since then. The result is that China's economy has expanded to roughly three times the size of India's in 2010—which has allowed China to invest in significantly in its military sector.[16] The Sino-India border dispute remains unresolved and continues to be a thorn in the side of bilateral relations. India's analysts fear a Chinese strategy of encirclement in Asia. This refers to China's numerous investment in building up ports facilities in the Indian Ocean, Such as at Bandar Abbas in Iran, Gwadar in Pakistan, Chittagong in Bangladesh and Hambantota in Sri Lanka.[17] China's rise in India' neighbourhood presents a sensitive challenge to Indian foreign policy, seen by some as deriving from the following calculus: 'Restricting India to the Asian Subcontinent remains China's policy.[18]

BILATERAL ISSUES : SRI LANKA, BANGLADESH, NEPAL

India's relation with other nations in its region are far from settled. India's hegemonic status—or at least perceived aspiration to it—creates threats perception among its smaller neighbour. They see India's military (and other) intervention in the neighbour countries in term of the outword projection and demonstration of military might'.[19] In the case of the Sri Lanka conflict, India's justification for military intervention were based on the security imperatives associated with the influx of Tamil refugees, the risk of disrupting commerce in the vital Palk straits, and the danger of external great powers involving themselves in the conflict, but India's military (formally peacekeeping) action proved counterproductive , alienating the Tamil Community, the LTTE, and the Sri Lanka government. Similarly India's action in 1971 in East Pakistan to relieve West Pakistan's military oppression, while justified in humanitarian terms and on the basis of massive refugee flow to India, was widely viewed as primarily an attempt to dismember an arch- rival. Moreover, contrary to India's expectations, its assistance to Bangladesh did not win an ally in the region: Bangladesh long provided safe haven for leaders of the United Liberation Front of Asom (ULFA), which operates in India's northeastern region.

While some in India saw the hand of Maoist in Nepal behind the early success of its own thriving multiple Maoist insurgencies, this is today farfetched. However high- handed India's past approach to Nepal has been , and however hostile Maoist in Nepal may have towards India, the Naxalite movement in India is home-grown and driven by local factors. It has developed today into the country's foremost internal security challenge.[20]

BILATERAL ISSUES : AFGHANISTAN

Aside from smaller nation such as Bhutan and Maldives, perhaps the one country in the region where India's involvement has not played against it—to the Pakistani establishment distress—is Afghanistan. India tend to see Delhi's policy as altruistic, in the words of a editorial: Delhi's partnership with Kabul has thrived because Delhi has neither geographic access to Afghanistan nor a political agenda of its own. What India wants is a moderate and a stable Afghanistan that is in harmony with its neighbours.'[21] This assessment glosses over a simple calculus in Delhi's policy towards Afghanistan to prevent Kabul from tilting excessively towards Pakistan, and allowing itself to be subsumed by Islamabad into its security space. Delhi worries that when the US-led NATO forces began to pull out, as several NATO members have signalled they wish to do soon, Kabul could submit to the combined influence of Pakistan (supported by China) and the Taliban , leaving India as the loser in a geostrategic tug-of-war.[22]

Addressing India's Security Challenges

Given the evolution of its domestic politics and foreign policy over the past six-odd years, what lessons can be drawn on India's ability to manage effectively key domestic and International security challenges? Sumit Ganguly relates the important challenges of 'developing a long-term strategic vision, one that is not subject to the vagaries of regime change, minor, adverse development in the country's immediate neighbourhood and periodic crisis' to the development of institutional mechanisms...and planning capabilites' he sees as different:

> *[India] has for the most part, been unable to develop a professional cadre of personal who are knowledge about questions of defence budgeting acquisition, capabilities and policy-making. The absence of such a body of skilled personnel has ill-served Indian defense policy-making, and has rendered decision subject to political whims and financial constraints.*[23]

One way of addressing some of India's security dilemmas, India's foreign policy would face several challenges and require a broader approach. Firstly, a clear articulation of the security and developmental objectives of the country will need to be done. The questions that arise are: what are India's primary security concerns? What is India's long-term strategy? What role does India seek in the immediate neighbourhood, in the extended neighbourhood, and at the global level? For this, a national debate and consensus would be required. Secondly, India would need to build the necessary institutions and capabilities to achieve these objectives. In particular, our decision-making structures will need to be revamped for greater transparency and effectiveness. Speedy decisions will be a must. Some specific challenges India's foreign policy will face are listed below.

a. India will need to have a strong, inclusive economy, a strong military, well-regulated borders and good governance to deal with the security and developmental challenges that it will face in the coming years.
b. India needs to develop comprehensive defence cooperation with friendly countries. This should include strategic linkages, training, capacity building, disaster management, etc. India could also fulfill the defence equipment needs of friendly countries. Defence diplomacy will assume importance in India's overall policy towards her neighbours.
c. There would be an increasing need to incorporate the human security concerns in foreign policy, which has traditionally been dominated by hard security concerns. The issues of water, food, energy, trade and investment, socio-economic and cultural contacts will assume greater salience in India's foreign policy. India would need to find abundant human, physical and financial resources to pursue a broad-based foreign policy with regard to its neighbours.
d. Terrorism, organised crime, human trafficking, cyber security and WMD proliferation will continue to pose challenges to India's security. Dealing with these will require an effective counter-terrorism policy, a forward-looking approach on cooperation with the neighbours to manage the borders, and including several new areas in regional cooperation agenda such as cyber security, science and technology, agricultural development, education culture, capacity-building, etc. Only by

adopting a holistic approach in which its neighbours and the people are involved, will help India meet the challenges of terrorism and of nontraditional security.[24]

e. India's security dilemmas is to lend greater consideration to strategic cooperation with the United States on regional security issues. Any suggestion of regional security cooperation with the U.S. runs against ideologues in Delhi harking back to non-alignment and realists questioning America's credibility as a long-term partner. Yet, it is possible to argue that it is in India's interest to seek out greater regional security cooperation with the United States. Two important reasons stand out. For one, despite the significant expansion of its own capabilities in the last two decades, India is not in a position to unilaterally contain Pakistan, reclaim regional primacy, and balance China. Second, any Indian strategy that focuses on producing these outcomes, rather than a rhetorical emphasis on ideological canon, would strengthen India's position by pooling its resources with that of another power that shares these interests. This is matter of power calculus and statecraft.[25]

CONCLUSION

India's security challenges are mostly structural in nature: Pakistan grievances, the China's threat and other challenges are likely to remain beyond India's exclusive control. It is thought that those challenges that are within reach, such as the economic exclusion of certain regions or ethnic groups, can be addressed through better allocation of the gain from economic growth.[26] Expanding economic relations can also provide a channel of cooperation with potential competitors or rivals. The region can progress if the countries of the region create interdependencies and cooperate with each other to tackle common challenges. India has a responsibility to promote cooperation as this will be its own national interest. The action that India takes today will have profound impact on the developments in the next 20 years, not only within India but also in the neighbourhood. India cannot control every development but, as a pre-eminent power in the region, its actions will have consequences. While new challenges will arise undoubtedly, a progressive foreign policy approach towards its neighbours—which places emphasis on people-to-people ties—is likely to be more effective. India will have to harness both its soft and hard powers judiciously.

Notes and References

1. Rumel Dhaiya, Ashok K. Behuria (eds.), '*India's Neighbourhood: Challenges in next two Decades*', Pentagon Press, New Delhi, 2012, p. 19.
2. Stanley A. Weiss, 'India, the Incredible and Vulnerable', *International Herald Tribune*, April 23, 2008.
3. Brain C. Schmidt, 'The Primacy of National Security', in Steve Smith, Amelia Hadfields and Tim Dunne (eds) *Foreign Policy: Theories, Actores, Cases*, United Kingdom: Oxford, 2012, pp. 188-89.
4. Vikram Sood, 'India and Regional Security Interest', in Alyssa Ayres and C. Raja Mohan (eds.) *Power Realignment in Asia: China, India, and the United State*, SAGE, New Delhi, 2009, p. 252.
5. Rajen Harshe, 'South Asian Regional Cooperation: Problems and Prospects', in Rajen Harshe and K.M. Seethi (eds) *Engaging with the World: Critical Reflection on India's Foreign Policy*, Orient Black Swan, New Delhi, 2009, p. 321.
6. Sood, p. 252.
7. Varun Sahni, '*The Agent—Structure Problem and India's External Security Policy*', in Navnita Chadha Behra (ed.) International Relations in South Asia, Search for an Alternative Paradigm, SAGE, New Delhi, 2008, pp. 212-13.
8. David M. Malone, '*Does the Elephant Dance? Contemporary Indian Foreign Policy*,' Oxford, New Delhi, 2011, p. 59.
9. J.N. Dixit, '*Across Borders: Fifty Years of India's Foreign Policy*', Picus Books, New Delhi, 1998, pp. 182-93.
10. International Crisis Group, '*Nepal's Trouble Tarai Region* , 'Asia Report No. 136, 9 July, 2007, p. 22.
11. Sugata Bose and Ayesha Jalal (eds.) Nationalism, Democracy and Development, Oxford University Press, New Delhi, 1997.
12. Malone, p. 60.
13. For a detail account of the various secessionist movements in the north-east, See Hussain '*Ethno-Nationalism and the Politics of Terror*', pp. 93-110.
14. Roland Buerk, 'Villagers left in limbo by border fence', *BBC News*, Dhaka, 28 January 2006, http://news.bbc.co.uk/2/hi/programmes/from_our_own_correspondent/4653810.stm .
15. C. Raja Mohan, 'Regional Security Challenges', cited in Seminar, 653-January 2014, p. 17.
16. For more Detail See http://data.worldbank.org/data-catalog/world-development-indicators/wdi-2010.
17. Sood, p. 260.
18. *Ibid.*, p. 261.
19. Harshe, pp. 321-2.

20. See Ashok Handoo, 'Naxal problem needs a holistic approach'; see also Asia Terrorism Portal www.satp.org/satporgtp/countries/india/moist/data_sheets/fatalitiesnaxal08.htm
21. 'The good Afghan', *Indian Expess*, 26 April, 2010.
22. Shishir Gupta, 'India shift Afghan Policy, ready to talk to Taliban', *Indian Express*, 29 March 2010.
23. Sumit Ganguly, 'Indian Defense Policy', in Niraja Gopal and Pratap Bhanu Mehta (eds.), The Oxford Companion to Politics in India, Oxford University Press, New Delhi, p. 550.
24. Rumel Dhaiya, Ashok K. Behuria (eds.), '*India's Neighbourhood: Challenges in next two Decades*', Pentagon Press, New Delhi, 2012, p. 218.
25. C. Raja Mohan, *'Regional Security Challenges'*, cited in Seminar, 653, January 2014, p. 19.
26. Malone, p. 74.

Gandhian Vision of Human Security

17

GHANSHYAM DEV

Right from the times of great Greek thinkers like Aristotle, the state was always considered to be a 'means' rather than an end. However, the 'end', was always a good life. But it seems very ridiculous that state-centric security has devoted whole of its might to protect the 'means' i.e., the state. Whereas, the 'end', i.e., a good life free from all types of insecurities had always been given a back seat. If we look at the borders of the states like US, China, India, etc., they look almost perfectly secure, but the question which arises here is; how much secure are their individual citizens as human beings? The mad race for armaments in order to be secure in terms of borders had left human beings even more insecure.

The state centric approach to security and the realist school in international relations led by authorities like Hans J. Morganthau and E.H. Carr with its roots in Machiavellian and Hobbesian tradition of human nature has given birth to a number of other insecurities rather than providing a true sense of security to the human civilization. Classical realism is primarily based on a pessimistic portrayal of human nature. Self-interested, competitive concerns with self preservation and lust for power are the basic assumption in the mutual intercourse among the various nations of the world according to the realist school. Therefore, this assumption leads to "struggle for power" among the nations of the world in order to maximize their national interest which is defined in terms of power. This conception and thinking has pushed the sovereign actions of the world towards a race to maximize their military strengths in order to make their borders more and more secure. However, the security of one nation has resulted into the increased insecurity of other nation/nations. This eventually leads the world to a mad race for armaments which has miserably failed to provide the security in the true sense of the term to the already strife-ridden world. More importantly, this state centric view of security has a very little concern about the human beings and human security. Now, the need of the hour is to replace the state-centric approach to security by human-centric approach.

It was Professor Mahbub-ul-Haq who first of all drew the attention of the world to the concept of Human security in UNDP Human Development Report (1994). UNDP Report originally argued that Human Security requires attention to both "freedom from fear" and "freedom from want". The human safety is to safeguard the vital core of all human lives from critical pervasive threats, in a way that is consistent with long term human fulfillment. Human security take its shape from human beings, vital core that is to be protected. Human security is deliberately protective. It recognizes that people and communities are fatally threatened by events well beyond their control.

Mahatma Gandhi has rightly said, "There is no way to peace, peace is the way". Gandhi was always in favour of pious means. For him, no 'end' can be justified which is achieved through unjust means because for him, "As you sow, so shall you reap". Security based on realistic approach through armaments or deterrence was never acceptable to Gandhi. State, for Gandhi was an evil; it is the embodiment of violence. By strengthening the armies and securing their borders, nations are still not in a position to provide lasting feeling of security to their citizens (human Beings). The threats to human security enlisted by UNDP, e.g., economic security, food security, health security, environmental security, personal security, community security, political security, etc. had already been addressed to in one form or the other by Mahatma Gandhi as back as during the first half of the last century. The problems of these threats to human security can be found catching the attention of Mahatma Gandhi in his writings and speeches. Not only that Gandhi has deliberated upon these eight problems of human security, he has rather gone a step further to talk of moral Swaraj which means moral independence and moral security which can be regarded as the highest type of security. Hence, the need of the hour is the look at the issue of security from the angle Mahatma wanted us to look at, i.e., from an angle which talks of lasting security based on peace and non-violence and achieved through pious means. Eventually what Gandhi wanted was security through peace and not peace through security.

Human insecurity is an ancient phenomenon. Threats of famine, war, drought, flood, wild animals, plague, and enslavement appear in ancient times across the world. Human insecurity, however painful, is not an historic anomaly. What has changed, and changed considerably, are the kinds of insecurity that people face, and the institutional possibilities of tempering that insecurity.

The particular phrase, "human security," is most often associated with the 1994 *Human Development Report* on Human Security, even though the term itself was in circulation earlier. The intent of human security is to bridge the freedom from want and freedom from fear. The battle of peace has to be fought on two fronts. The first is the security front where victory spells freedom from fear.

The second is the economic and social front where victory means freedom from want. Only victory on both fronts can assure the world of an enduring peace.

The phrase 'freedom from fear' is intended to indicate freedom from violence, and the phrase 'freedom from want', freedom from poverty. It is important to bear this mental equation in mind, because of course people also fear poverty and destitution; they also want peace and protection. The 1994 *Human Development Report* was also explicitly crafted as an agenda for the Social Summit in Copenhagen, at which extensive discussion of the peace dividend was held and emphasized their central concern with human beings. In the final analysis, human security is a child who did not die, a disease that did not spread, a job that was not cut, an ethnic tension that did not explode in violence, a dissident who was not silenced. Human security is not a concern with weapons — it is a concern with human life and dignity.

In a slightly more systematic mode, the report identified the following four essential characteristics of human security:

Human security is a universal concern. It is relevant to people everywhere, in rich nations and poor. The components of human security are interdependent. Human security is easier to ensure through early prevention than later intervention. It is less costly to meet these threats upstream than downstream. Human security is people-centred. It is concerned with how people live and breathe in a society, how freely they exercise their many choices, how much access they have to market and social opportunities–and whether they live in conflict or in peace.

Finally, the 1994 UNDP report defined human security as:

1) Safety from chronic threats such as hunger, disease and repression.
2) Protection from sudden and hurtful disruptions in the patterns of daily life–whether in jobs, in homes or in communities.

The report developed this definition in relation to seven dimensions of human security: personal, environmental, economic, political, community, health, and food security. The report argued for deliberate actions to provide human security during economic crises, as well as to reduce other causes of human insecurity such as global crime, environmental degradation, and communication that threatens cultural diversity.

The key premises of the report are : (i) its joint focus on freedom from fear and freedom from want; and (ii) its four emphases on universality, interdependence, prevention, and people-centeredness. These formed, and continue to shape, human security discussions.

Human security in its broadest sense embraces far more than the absence of violent conflict. It encompasses human rights, good governance, access to education and health care and ensuring that each individual has opportunities and choices to fulfil his or her own potential. Every step in this direction is also a step towards reducing poverty, achieving economic growth and preventing conflict. Freedom from want, freedom from fear and the freedom of future generations to inherit a healthy natural environment–these are the interrelated building blocks of human–and therefore national security.

It is quite important to work out carefully the relationship between human security and state security. One key reason is that the United Nation's "existing organizational mandates and mechanisms draw heavily from state security assumptions." Another key reason is that collaboration with state security forces would be essential to human security at the national level. Also grave threats to state security evoke well-funded, emphatic, expert responses. In the face of security threats, groups that otherwise differ on many niceties will rally and support joint action. And nations regularly invest considerable resources in anticipation of security threats, which range from the doctoral research of engineers to the daily callisthenics that maintain the musculature of army troops. As a result, state security issues are associated in many minds with effective response mechanisms. These characteristics of funding, research, consensus, efficacy, and "get-to-the-bottom-of-the-matter" attention are also necessary to confront the grave threats to human security.

Furthermore, human security may be a timely extension of the state security framework, one which explores and develops the newer issues that are already on the edges of the security agenda, and brings outside expertise to bear on issues that already have the attention and concern of national security advisors.

Security not only advocates investment in education as part of the national security strategy, but also relates the material well-being and the worldwide expansion of material abundance and the eradication of poverty. It should also promote political pluralism, freedom of thought and speech, and individual liberty. There are no guarantees against violence and evil in the world. We believe, nonetheless, that the expansion of human rights and basic material well-being constitutes a sturdy bulwark against them.

The broadening scope of state security has also been reflected in the emergence of terms such as "common," and "collective" and "global" to modify "security." Common Security is "inclusive of but extending beyond the human dimensions of military conflict—incorporating health and population dimensions of political, ethnic, economic and environmental security as well." Collective Security, refers to a system in which each state in the system accepts that the security of one is the concern of all, and agrees to join in a collective response to aggression. Global security must be broadened from its traditional focus on the security of states to include the security of people and the planet.

Three changes can be identified: The first is that many more "fundamental" issues are on the agenda about the various possible security configurations. For example, would a collective security system be feasible or desirable or is this a period of transition to a situation of rivalry between a different set of powers. The agenda of human security likewise raises fundamental issues about the international order, both because some global threats to human security may best be addressed by international institutions, and because security concerns are also being undertaken by NGOs and by local and regional groups. The second change is that security studies has "a fresh and full agenda."

Finally, it is "a more scholarly agenda." This reflects the increasing need for a strong conceptual framework and a clear methodology in order to manage effectively the increase in relevant institutions and in security agendas—a need that is shared in human security. The ongoing developments of conceptions of national security clearly overlap with the human security agenda.

There are also key differences between state and human security. One regards an issue of presentation or of substance in the human security agenda. Traditionalists ... have little patience with those who would dilute the established field of security studies by overloading it with an ambitious agenda of problems and issues that would compromise the analytical power of their critical ideas. Human security advocates are cast as offering the promise of a new, more cooperational, but perhaps unattainable and unrealistic international order. One writer went so far as to associate human security with liberals who believe "human nature is essentially good and peace loving." To many in national security, it seems that human security lies at the outer edge of liberal internationalism, remote in relevance, ideal rather than reliable, and undisciplined by the burden of accountability and responsibility that national security advisors regularly shoulder.

A key conceptual difference between state security and human security is the populations under consideration. State agencies by definition have a different responsibility to the citizenry than they do to international populations at large. This difference is by no means a deficiency. Yet it does require clarity of the grounds for obligation to citizens outside the nation-state. One set of possible justifications is that the expansion of human rights and basic material well-being constitutes a sturdy bulwark against violence and evil. That is, protecting others' human security strengthens the security of national populations and thus would be in the self-interest of the nation-state, because it would be significantly less costly than countering violence or terrorism. The problem with this logic of course is that interest in human security might swiftly cease if more cost-effective terrorism prevention mechanisms were discovered. A more durable justification would be that all nations have an imperfect obligation to address breaches of human security. The case for responsibility for non-citizens must be made to state entities (as well as to individuals and groups within states), and it matters how it is made.

Second, state security has at least one additional objective that is distinct from human security. For a characteristic aim of foreign policy in the realist theory, which is also *a de facto* aim in many nations, is to *maximize* the state's power. Thus national security is also substantially concerned with the relative distribution of power between states, and with territorial integrity. That concern is legitimate and lively worldwide. However, it is not part of the human security agenda. In theory, the human security agenda could be realized, so long as human beings enjoyed security of their core vital functions in a way that was consistent with their long-term fulfilment, the human security agenda could be said to be complete.

The concept of human development refers to the broad approach to expanding people's choices or capabilities not only in terms of income, but also in areas such as health, education, technology, the environment, employment. The human development school, emerged in the 1990s, building on a series of previous reactions against the dominant paradigm of economic development, which took economic growth maximization as its objective. Growth, it was argued, was insufficient as an objective, since aggregate growth could be realized alongside less desirable states such as wrenching deprivation among the poor, political oppression, or environmental degradation. The route of alternatives to economic growth as the standard bearer of development has a forceful history of several decades.

The goals of human development, which evolved out of the basic human needs approach, were general and could apply to any country,. regardless of where it lay on the spectrum of wealth or poverty, of crime or stability, of peace or war. Human development clearly holds that socio-economic policies should focus on people and their well-being as the final objective, rather than focusing on economic growth or any other state of affairs as ends in themselves. While the Human Development Index, which is a well-known by-product of this approach, explicitly includes health and education as well as income, the human development approach is not limited to these sectors but rather focuses on human choice and freedom *per se*. Human development is a process of enlarging people's choices. Enlarging people's choices is achieved by expanding human capabilities and functionings.

The change from development aimed at relieving material poverty and providing for basic needs to development aimed at "giving people choices" also came about in response of the impetus to highlight the importance of dignity, esteem and other non-material aspects of life.

Given this sketch of human development, it may now be evident that human development and human security share four fundamental perspectives: they are people-centred; they are multi-dimensional; they have broad views on human fulfilment in the long term; and they address chronic poverty.

First, human security and human development are both people-centred. Both understand people to be "ends" and not "means". This emphasis has led both to challenge dominant paradigms that take instrumental or technical achievements (national security, economic growth) as an end or objective, because these technical achievements may go alongside deeply undesirable states of affairs. Furthermore, the dominant paradigms do not have a role for 'bottom-up' human agency (and understanding people as ends means understanding them not only as objects but also as agents). In both cases, criticism of the dominant paradigm has been far from uncontroversial. While the logic (of 'people-centredness') may seem simplistic, in both the development community and the security community, the struggle to communicate the relevance, practicality, and importance of looking beyond purely instrumental or technical considerations, has been considerable and is ongoing.

Second, both human development and human security are multi-sectoral and multidimensional undertakings. Both address people's dignity as well as their material and physical concerns.

The measures of success go beyond income and preparedness. This breadth complicates the approaches, and makes priority-setting a key concern. At the same time, because the task of discussing and setting priorities (amid disagreement) forms an explicit part of the human security and human development approaches, both approaches are able to adapt constantly to new scenarios and new threats.

Third, human development provides the "broad picture" long-term objective of human fulfillment within any society, whether it is rich or whether it is poor; whether composed of refugees or artisans or farmers. This broad objective is shared by human security although the human security approach pursues a narrower agenda. In fact the phrase "in a manner that is consistent with long term human fulfilment" that appears in the working definition of human security could be rephrased as 'in a manner that is consistent with long-term human development.'

Fourth, human development and human security both address chronic poverty. That is, human development is a broad approach that is relevant for rich and for poor persons and communities. But when the human development approach is applied to impoverished persons who already live with chronic insecurity of food or health or livelihood, it overlaps with and may be indistinguishable from human security. For this subset of persons—the chronic poor/insecure – human security and human development processes (which include participation) are likely to identify and prioritise the same capabilities. And the same types of policy recommendations, such as girls' education, freedom of the press, and preventative health care, are likely to emerge. And it is in this context Gandhian vision of Human Security becomes relevant and urgent. Gandhi tackled this problem in his own characteristic way. In his opinion:-

State: Threat to Human Security, The first and most basic principle applicable is that human security forms a part of the international dialogue, and has to be subjected to the same criteria as have been used to promote this dialogue by tradition and general acceptance. This means state security and human security should not be put in opposition without good reason, that the first effort should be to advance human security by cooperative means. Some have suggested that the state itself is the primary threat to human security. The creation and defence of the Westphalian state form is at the heart of regional insecurity. This view clearly goes too far in asking for intervention as the first choice, is at least for the time being not acceptable within the kind of paradigm that is taking shape. Further, power in international relations continues to maintain the salience it has enjoyed for centuries. While outlining the human security construct in a way that brings closer an agenda for action, we cannot pretend that in the post Cold War world the role of the state, once expressed primarily through military, political and economic power, and now increasingly expressed, as a supplement, through the power of the concept of human security, is about to be abandoned; or that the importance of power has disappeared. This is precisely what Gandhi preached.

State as an engine of violence: Gandhi was also very much suspicious of the power of the state. Gandhi regarded the state as the organization of violence. While Marx and engels regard the state as the agent of the exploiting classes. Tolstoy and Gandhi consider it as the engine of violence. Gandhi was the protagonist of a divine kingdom on earth and hence, necessarily, he was repelled by the resort to force by political institutions. He has in mind the ultimate vision of the perfection of mankind and hence he is hostile to the modern state which, to him, is a mechanical structure representing organized and concentrated violence. Unlike St. Augustine and other Christian political thinkers, he did not regard political force as the divinely appointed punishment or remedy for the sins of man. Nor did he regard social and political associations and the state as the actualization and objectivization of universal reason or the revelations of all an all-pervasive Spirit. He is not conservative historicist so as to identify the existing institutional mechanism with the realized realm of free-will. Neither does he regard the state as being almost the second nature of the individual in the external world. Nor is he an exponent of the servile cult of state omnipotence.

There is no element of moral spontaneity in the state. Hence, Gandhi had no love for the organized institutions of political power. He accepted, instead, the worth of the plasticity and spontaneity generated by non-violence. The compulsiveness of the commands of the state leads to the destruction of the plasticity and subtlety of personality. Hence Gandhi said: "I look upon an increase in the power of the State with the greatest fear, because, although while apparently doing good by minimizing exploitation, it does the greatest harm to mankind by destroying individuality, which lies at the root of all progress." This is what a large number of exponent of human security are advocating.

The second principle is that while the borders, there should be just a few simple rules about the way security intersects with the other disiciplines involved like humanitarian law, human rights, gender studies etc. There is so far no sign of inter-subjective agreement on such rules. When does poverty, for instance, become a human security problem? There is need to be for a start, some recognizable features of traditional security analysis in the effort to securities anything. There has to be a present existential or a real future anticipated threat in the field concerned, and the threat should be sufficiently grave of emergency action of an extreme kind to be taken; normal methods should not apply.

In the economic sector, as an example, should the possible closure of an industry be treated as a matter of security? The liberal economy treats the rise and fall of the private corporate sector as part of the day to day business of life, something which cannot be securitized, but if a large and important sector is affected, say if the power supply substantially shuts down, there is a case for securitizing. While the inter-subjective process is at a beginning threats to collectivities other than the state could also be incorporated through rules. Included could also be threat to the survival of the collective unit concerned, the minority, tribe or linguistic group, or to an integral element of their being, such as their economy, culture or way of life. In other words, seasonal water shortages, a temporary fall in the availability of food grains, sporadic incidents of crime and similar problems which are common to many societies cannot be included without rendering the concept meaningless from the viewpoint of action by the international community. Another difficult issue is prioritization, whether the environment should get more attention than poverty, health than education, and so on. These are the key issues which Gandhi have a definite opinion similar to those expressed by human security.

The third principle is that the concept must have an international locus. Te promotion of human security in a particular situation should be susceptible to agreement by the international community that has a responsibility in the matter. There is, in fact, a widening spectrum of developments which happen in one country but which concerns others through international relief efforts that need to be mounted, or the work of NGOs or a donor-recipient

	Traditional Security	*Human Security (Gandhian Vision)*
Referent	Traditional security policies are designed to promote demands ascribed to the state. Other interests are subordinated to those of the state. Traditional security protects a state's boundaries, people, institutions and values.	Human security is people-centered. Its focus shifts to protecting individuals. The important dimensions are to entail the well-being of individuals and respond to ordinary people's needs in dealing with sources of threats
Scope	Traditional security seeks to defend states from external aggression. *Walter Lippmann* explained that state security is about a state's ability to deter or defeat an attack. It makes uses of deterrence strategies to maintain the integrity of the state and protect the territory from external threats	In addition to protecting the state from external aggression, human security would expand the scope of protection to include a broader range of threats, including environmental pollution, infectious diseases, and economic deprivation
Actor(s)	The state is the sole actor, to ensure its own survival. Decision making power is centralized in the government, and the execution of strategies rarely involves the public. Traditional security assumes that a sovereign state is operating in an anarchical international environment, in which there is no world governing body to enforce international rules of conduct.	The realization of human security involves not only governments, but a broader participation of different actors viz. regional and international organizations, non-governmental organizations and local communities
Means	Traditional security relies upon building up national power and military defense. The common forms it takes are armament races, alliances, strategic boundaries etc.	Human security not only protects, but also empowers people and societies as a means of security. People contribute by identifying and implementing solutions to insecurity

relationship. But the areas of disagreement are also wide, human rights, refugees, and the use of resources being examples. Hence, two things are required for this international locus. A set of universally acceptable values, and an agreed pattern of implementing international action, through fire-fighting or long term peace building.

This leads one from Nationalism to Internationalism. Gandhi was intensely attached to the concept of Indian Nationalism. But he was also an internationalist and always emphasized his role as a citizen of the world. He was a great national leader but he was also unsurpassed in modern times as a lover of humanity. In Gandhi, despite his nationalist preoccupations the dominant concepts were, always truth, non-violence and purity and, hence, as a believer in positive love for man he believed in internationalism and in the essential unity of man. The South Africa and Indian politics had been the laboratories in which he "experimented" with his formulae of truth and non-violence which are indeed universal values. There is, thus, indeed, a supreme humanitarian standpoint in Gandhi. He was a great fighter for Swaraj but they would consider human welfare to be a matter of greater concern. He fought against the British empire but he loved the British people. He considered no person to be an enemy because beyond the sovereignty of the nation he looked to the categorical imperative of human brotherhood. He absolutely believed in a union of hearts-homonia-of all men and women of the world.

Gandhi's internationalism was only a sociological and political application of the great norm of Ahimsa which means universal non-hatred and non-violence. Buddha and St. Francis showed the tenderest care for the meanest creatures of the world. Their love extended also to the animal kingdom. Gandhi, like them, believed in the doctrine of absolute and universal compassion for all living beings. A believer in God naturally has the feeling of identity with all creatures because all are the creations of God. Gandhi was never tired of repeating that men could receive divine grace and affection only if they loved their brethren. He said: "We are all tarred with the same brush; we are all members of the vast human family." Hence love of the human kind was only an aspect of his ahimsa, and internationalism is a concrete means to realize at the political level, the universal love for humanity.

But Gandhi wanted that before cosmopolitanism and internationalism could become a reality, those countries which were still suffering under feudal overlordship and colonial dependence should have the political freedom to determine their own future. He, therefore, cried for a halt to the nefarious game of imperial "gengsterism" among nations. Nationalism, this, though only a stage, was a very important one towards the realization of internationalism. He asked: "How is this vast mass of humanity to be a flame in the cause of world deliverance, unless and until it has touched and felt freedom", India had first to be free before she could co-operate on terms of equality with other nations. Hence, it is clear that Gandhi's romantic conception of the soul of a nation was not meant as the psychological support to the virulent national chauvinism but was only a means to extol the soul of a people against the effective organizations and combinations of imperialistic power that may attempt to suppress rising nationalism. The units that could form any international union should do that from their own will and this implied the previous attainment of national sovereignty by them. Hence Gandhi wrote: "It is impossible for one to be internationalist without being a nationalist. Internationalism is possible only when nationalism becomes a fact, i.e., when people belonging to different countries have organized themselves and are able to act as one man."

In an obvious criticism of the League of Nations based on the concept of the great powers' predominance, Gandhi had written that an international league could really exist, "Only when all the nations, big or small, composing it are fully independent." Nationalism would not mark the climax of human security; it was not an end but a stage. He, hence, stood only for nationalism that was health-giving, religious and therefore humanitarian. He felt that Indian nationalism should be a step towards internationalism and human unity. He was also of the opinion that India's freedom could be deserved only if there was good will towards the whole of the human family.

He wanted India to be a free nation in order that she could sacrifice herself for the service of mankind. Hence, he wrote, "I want the freedom of my country so that other countries may learn something from my free country, so that the resources of my country may be utilized for the benefit of mankind. Just as the cult of patriotism teaches us today that the individual has to die for the family, the family has to die for the village, the village for the country; even so a country has to be free in order that it may die, if necessary, for the benefit of the world. My love, therefore, or nationalism or my idea of nationalism is that my country may become free, that if need be the whole of the country may die, so that the human race may live. There is no room for race hatred there. Let that be our nationalism."

Nationalism was thus not the pinnacle of human endeavours but was only a stage in the political evolution of man. Through national consolidations it was possible to get over the obstacles of caste, group and local prejudices, conflicts and struggles. Thus nationalism could become a means to political and psychological integration. Once, local and sectional hatreds had been consumed by the fire of nationalism, the time would naturally come when the nation would sacrifice itself for the good of the world. Gandhi wrote: "My patriotism includes the good of mankind in general. Therefore, my service of India includes the service of humanity. The whole scheme for the liberation of India is based upon the development of internal strength. It is a plan of self-purifications." He wanted that Indian nationalism should mean the development of the national strength of India so that renovated India could serve mankind. Hence there could be no place for the pursuit of national interest to the detriment of the legitimate rights of other nations, according to the tenets of Gandhian foreign policy, which believed that the destiny of India lay not in militarization but in the realization of the noble mission of friendship and peace in the world. Thus we see that Gandhism teaches the conception of transcendence of narrow, exclusive, aggressive and chauvinistic nationalism and affirms the fundamental proposition that one's good consists in the good of mankind. Gandhi's conception of internationalism, thus, is an effective theoretical counterbalance to the almost blind adherence to the cult of national patriotism and absolute sovereignty which we find in Hegelianism, and fascism. Thus, if on the one side he was trenchant critic of western imperialism and a fighter for "Purna Swaraj", he would refuse to regard the nation-state as the final category in the political evolution of man.

Gandhi visualized a plan of humanity unity to be realized by the federal organization of friendly interdependent states. He had a great devotion to the noble goal of international co-operation and universal harmony, because, according to him, not to believe in the possibility of "permanent peace" amounts to disbelief in the "Godliness of human nature". Hence he wanted that permanent peace should be secured. He also pleaded for world order and world federation. He wrote: "Isolated independence is not the goal of the world states. It is voluntary interdependence. The better mind of the world desires today not absolutely independent states warring one against another, but a federation of friendly interdependent states. The consummation of that event may be far off. I want to make no grand claim for our country. But I see nothing grand or impossible about our expressing our readiness for universal interdependence rather than independence. I desire the ability to be totally independent without asserting the independence." In a note addressed to Maurice Frydman on 28th July, 1942, Gandhi has asserted his faith in a federally organized world-state. If I can get freedom for India through non–violent means, power of non-violence is firmly established, empire idea dissolves and the World-State takes its place in which all the states of the world are free and equal, no state has its military. There may be a world police to keep order in the absence of universal belief in non-violence.

On July 4, 1947, at a prayer speech Gandhi visualized that "if by India's effort such a world federation of free and independent states was brought into being, the hope of the kingdom of God, otherwise called Ram Raj, might legitimately be entertained."

He agreed that the only condition for the survival of world civilization was the realization of world union under one central governing body composed of representatives of the constituent entities. Most probably, Gandhi had in mind the federal pattern for this central governing body."

Gandhi would like the world government to non-cooperate with the lawless, aggressive and recalcitrant forces. But a world police force may be necessary in the beginning. This police force, under the control of world authority, would exercise its power only as the last sanction when moral and non-violent sanctions had ceased to have effect. This is the ultimate for human security.

References

Adam Roberts and Benedict Kingsbury (eds.), United Nations, Divided World: The UN's Role In International Relations, New Expanded Edition (Oxford: Oxford University Press), 1993.

Barry Buzan, Ole Waever, and Jaap de Wilde, Security: A New Framework of Analysis (Boulder: Lynne Rienner), 1998.

Beales, A.C.F., The History of Peace (London: London Press), 1931.

Blatz, William Ernest, Human Security: Some Reflections (London: University of London Press), 1967.

Booth, K. (ed.), Critical Security Studies and World Politics (Boulder, Co: Lynne Rienner), 2005.

Fischer, Louis, Gandhi: His Life and Message for the World (New York: Vintage Books), 1954.

Gandhi, M.K., An Autobiography or The Story of My Experiments with Truth (Ahmedabad: Navajivan Publishing House), 1983.

Gandhi, M.K., Hind Swaraj or Indian Home Rule (Ahmedabad: Navajivan Publishing House), 1983.

Gandhi, M.K., Constructive Programme: Its Meaning and Place (Ahmedabad: Navajivan Press), 1945.

Hampson, Fen Osler, with Jean Daudelin, John B. Hay, Todd Martin, and Holly Reid, Madness in the Multitude: Human Security and World Disorder (Ottawa: Oxford University Press), 2002.

Human Security Centre, Human Security Report Project (Vancouver: The University of British Columbia), 2008.

King, Gary and Christopher Murray, "Rethinking Human Security", *Political Science Quarterly,* Volume 116, Number 4, 2001-02.

Majid Tehranian (ed.), Worlds Apart: Human Security and Global Governance (London and New York), 1999.

United Nations Development Programme's (UNDP) Human Development Report, 1994.

The Concept of Human Security 18

ANU SHARMA

Security is a universal concern. Right from the time of birth till death the concern for security remains of crucial importance to human beings. Food, woman, land, property, etc. had been the major reasons for attack on man for which he had to keep himself secure during ancient and primitive times. During the next stage, man had to fight for the security of his family, clan and the tribe. Ushering into the modern period and the age of nation state, the concern for national security became of utmost importance which finally resulted into world wars and a mad race for armament.

The basic thing which is to be noted here is that security is not a new concept in social sciences. In fact, security is the essential ingredient of the international system around which nation states originated and sustained. But modern concept of human security identifies the inherent weakness of this traditional security paradigm which basically focuses on security of the state instead of security of individual. The dominant concept of security, traditionally, was state centric, extending support and legitimacy to instruments of states and upholding the principle of state sovereignty. Plato's 'Ideal State', Aristotle's 'Statesman', Hobbes' 'Leviathan', Machiavelli's 'Prince and above all Marxian concept of 'Dictatorship of the Proletariat' highlight the ultimate goal or end of state as security and protection of individual and community, even though they have different views about the means to attain this goal. But neither of these theories gave an independent identity and existence to human security nor did they develop conceptual framework on human security. Instead security was conceived as an integral part of national security which put emphasis on military centric solutions to security related issues. Even though the UN system was established to protect security of the people, the UN principle for security was initially focused on ways in which the structures and practices of the modern state might address threats to its sovereignty

In this context it is important to examine the origin and various stages of development of human security both as a concept and tool for implementation. Since human security lacks conceptual clarity and an exclusive paradigm for intellectual discourse, it is difficult to analyze the historical development of the concept with precision and clarity. Human security does not have specific borderlines. Anything which affects the security of individual and collective existence may come under human security. It was UNDP Human Development Report 1994, which, for the first time, explicitly articulated the importance of human security as tool of policy making and implementation. Simultaneously, Canada, Japan and Norway proposed human security centric governance initiatives in domestic and foreign policy options. However, while analyzing the origin and development of the concept it is impertinent to go beyond the UN interpretations and recent policy debates. Concerns towards human security and to critically examine the traditional state centric security, centric notions were attempted even during the cold war era, though it was not universally accepted and discussed. Hence, the following discussion is an attempt to analyze the development of the concept and it has been divided it into three stages - Pre-Cold War Era, Cold War Era and Post-Cold War Era.

HUMAN SECURITY IN PRE-COLD WAR ERA

During this period security of individual and society was not unknown in social sciences in general and political theory in particular. The core stream of thought in western political theory right from Socrates to Harold Laski and Mcpherson focused on the best governance system which provides security, well-being and opportunities to individual and community. In economics also welfare economists criticized classical growth centric models of development and highlighted the need for interlinking human welfare and economics. Aftêr the decline of feudalism and emergence of nation states, primary responsibility of maintaining security was vested with state which ultimately led to linking all notions of security with territorial integrity and national sovereignty. In this classical formulation, security is about how state uses force to counter threats to their territorial integrity, their autonomy and their domestic political order primarily from other states and anti state actors within state. This classical national security formulation has been criticized on various grounds. It restricts the scope of security to military threats. In this view rival states may deploy other kinds of threats against each others territorial integrity and domestic political order.

Thus, in conventional security perspective, security was not associated with other form of threats and fear. With the advent of Marxism and rise of trade unions demanding more share and equal distribution of resources, some states including USA initiated social security policies not as a means to protect human security but as a tactful strategy of containment of communism. Thus even in 19th century and first part of the 20th century the dominant concept of security was state centric privileging the instruments and agents of the state carrying forward the principles of state sovereignty as first articulated in the Treaty of Westphalia in 1648.

After the First World War also the two dominant strands of foreign policy—economic development and military security—did not address the core issues which threaten the existence of human beings including growing poverty, displacement, migration, armed conflicts, environmental degradation etc. witnessed balance of power, formation of alliances and arms race focusing blindly on the conventional dimension of military security. This unilateral approach to security ultimately resulted in Second World War and the human catastrophe in Hiroshima and Nagasaki.

The post-World War period witnessed significant transformation in international socio-economic-political configuration. This was the period when process of decolonization started with the result of newly formed independent nation states in Asia and Africa, displacement and rehabilitation of refugees, reconstruction of war affected countries etc. raised the limitations of conventional military centric approach to address human problems and highlighted the need for redefined strategies and policies. The UN was born into such a world emerging out of the shadows of war and hitherto unimagined destruction. It was founded on the ideals of peace justices with an international system of law and procedure that would replace military aggression and war with negotiation and collective security. Although the UN was fundamentally constructed around the concept of national sovereignty, from the very start the security of people was of equal importance. The UN Charter itself states: "We the people of the UN determined to save succeeding generations from the scourge of war which twice in our life time has brought untold sorrow to mankind...'

However here also UN did not give much attention to the non-political aspects of human security and instead give emphasis on protection of state sovereignty rather than individual or community security. Threats which affect people irrespective of national boarders, territorial limits, geographical location etc were least addressed. More over the functional pattern of nation states were identified in terms of pursuit of power. It was this realist approach and militaristic interpretation which determined the nature of security paradigm during the cold war period.

HUMAN SECURITY DURING COLD WAR ERA

In the context of the above mentioned global realities and escalating threats to human existence, there was a general consensus with the international community that the United Nations Charter did not sufficiently define the essential human rights it referenced. A universal declaration that specified the rights of individuals was felt necessary and was ultimately made through Universal Declaration of Human Rights in December 1948. The declaration recognizes inherent dignity and equal and inalienable rights of all members of the human family. It further protects right to life, liberty and security of person, inhuman or degrading treatment or punishment to name a few. This ratification was indeed the first step towards making universal acceptance of certain rights and human security related issues. Although the Charter does not provide any concrete strategy for implementing the rights, it still provides a beacon light for the further development of human security.

Another event which should be mentioned while discussing the historical development of human security is efforts of international community towards disarmament and nuclear non-proliferation. NPT of 1968, Anti Ballistic Missile Treaty of 1972, etc. led to establishing certain universally acceptable norms and regulations to curb these threats associated with weapons of mass destruction. Unlike the traditional notions the step towards disarmament gives more emphasis on human security rather than state sovereignty. This altered concept was essential especially in the context of Vietnam War, Cuban crisis and the increasing propensity to use force and aggression as a means to protect national security. Thus we may say that international disarmament initiatives, partly, deviate from traditional security paradigm and conceive human security connotations.

In the post-colonial period, the newly emerged countries in Africa Asia and Latin America started facing new set of problems like extreme poverty, over population, mal-nutrition, industrial backwardness, civil war, ethnic conflicts, epidemics etc. Although these problems were already existing in these countries during colonial rule but remained un-addressed due to colonial powers' dominance and could not surface in public domain. Traditional framework of state and national security was not adequate enough to address these post colonial social and economic issues effectively. Even though developed countries extended their financial aid and intervention to tackle the problems of under developed countries, it did not succeed well because their methodology was growth centric rather than development centric. In this context, a group of development theorists including Samir Amin, Gunder Frank and Franz Fennen, put forward alternative approaches to development, focusing on equal distribution of resources and income. This new paradigm in development economics interlinked security of individual with proper share in resource allocation which ultimately enlarged the scope of human security. As Kanti Bajpai rightly commented 'the genealogy of the idea of human security can be related to if not traced back to the growing dissatisfaction with prevailing notions of development and security in the 60s, 70s and 80s. Economics undoubtedly led the way with its critiques of the dominant models of economic development beginning in the 60s'.

In the 70s, another attempt was made to address the core questions of human security through the World Order Models Project [WOMP] which gave importance to normative challenges to existing system of state centric security regime. The central feature of the normative challenge that is proposed rests on an acceptance of human solidarity and all its implications especially a shared responsibility to seek equity and dignity for every person on the planet without regard to matters of national identity or territorial boundary. WOMP requires a structural relevance based on the four value positions of peace, economic equity, social and political justice, and ecological balance.

Since 1970s the literature on human centric governance and development policies began to enrich social science research and practice. These group of scholars and various international commissions played vital role in conceptualizing human security both at theoretical and application level. First among these intellectual efforts was made from the Club of Rome Group founded in 1968 by Aurelio Peccei, an Italian industrialist, and Alexander King, a Scottish scientist. It raised considerable public attention with its report *Limits to Growth,* which has sold 30 million copies in more than 30 translations, making it the best selling environmental book in world history. In this book they identified certain issu s which may affect the survival of the world itself irrespective of national boundaries and cultural specificities. The book used the World 3 model to simulate the consequence of interactions between the Earth's and human systems. The World 3 model was a computer simulation of interactions among population, industrial growth, food production and limits in the ecosystems of the Earth. Five variables were examined in the original model, on the assumption that exponential growth accurately described their patterns of increase. These variables are: world population, industrialization, pollution, food production and resource depletion. The Club of Rome Reports noted that:

"Every person in the world faces a series of pressures and problems that require his attention and action. These problems affect him at many different levels. He may spend much of his time trying to find tomorrow's food ... He may be concerned about personal power or the power of the nation in which he lives. He may worry about a world war ... or a war next week with a rival clan in his neighborhood." In short, the group proposed that there was a complex global system influencing the individual's life chances and that there were alternative ways of conceptualizing global development and, ultimately, global security so as to sustain and improve those life chances. Thus, Club of Rome and World 3 model popularized some crucial threats under which human beings live and thus provided solid foundation to human security dynamics in domestic and international public policy.

Willy Brandt Commission of 1978 and his report known as North South Report [1980] also occupies significant role in conceptualizing human security. The title of the report itself reads: To ensure survival, The Brandt Report seeks a balance in developmental policies and demands that the countries of the South be integrated into the global economic system. The North-South Commission expects that this will bring about needed improvements in economic and social conditions in disadvantaged countries. At the same time, the rich industrial countries of the North are called upon to share their means and power with the countries of the South. The Report contains a number of proposals for the reform and transformation of the world economic system. It concludes that the introduction of such a new system would be an important contribution to the survival of humanity. In his introduction to the report, Brandt wrote: "Our Report is based on what appears to be the simplest common interest: that mankind wants to survive, and one might even add has the moral obligation to survive. This not only raises traditional questions of peace and war, but also tries how to overcome world hunger, mass misery and alarming disparities between the living conditions of rich and poor. Thus North South Report made the discourse on security much wider inclusive and highlight the need for incorporating the humane centric agenda in global policy framework.

Another important milestone is Olof Palme Commission Report on Disarmament and Security Issues. The Palme Commission issued the 1982 report, Common Security, which argued that both East and West have legitimate security needs. It can never be possible, the Commission said, to demand unilateral security for one block based on superior military resources. On the contrary, in a world of incomprehensibly destructive nuclear potential, every ideological offence towards military supremacy is a threat to universal security. Apart from his focus on disarmament and international security the report also gives importance to security threats faced by Third World countries from poverty, hunger deprivation and economic inequalities.

The initiatives of Brandt and Palme in popularizing the concept of a common universal security and the linkages between security and disarmament was further upheld by Iga Thorssen in her report submitted to UN in 1982. Presenting her expert report on Disarmament and development to UN she concluded that the world can either continue to pursue the arms race with characteristic vigor or move consciously and with deliberate speed towards a more stable and balanced social and economic development within a more sustainable international economic and political order. It cannot do both.

The above analysis presents various stages and implications of security before evolving itself into a theoretical construct of human security. It is evident that during the cold war period security was essentially state centric even though attempts were made to give an inclusive and comprehensive concept of security involving issues of environment, poverty development and disarmament. Thus the intellectual stimulation expressed through commission reports together with institutional mechanisms initiated by UN disarmament policies, strengthened the efforts towards universal security cutting across regions and races.

Another important contribution of this period is that scholars and policy makers began to recognize that even successful examples of territorial security don't necessarily ensure the security of citizens within state. With Robert McNamara and Brandt, analysts also began to recognize environmental degradation and natural disasters such as epidemics floods earthquakes and drought as important threats to security as much as human made military disasters. These debates thus provided a strong platform for human security to emerge with an independent identity. The process was further encouraged by the power-shift in global politics necessitated through collapse of USSR, fall of Berlin wall and ultimately the end of cold war.

The inclusion of the human security concept in the debate has much to do with long-standing dissatisfaction with state-centric approaches among critical security scholars and with the post-Cold War reorientation towards intra-state security, the site of much human insecurity. Beyond the conceptual challenges that it presents to the state-centric understanding of security, human security is championed by many scholars and practitioners concerned with the human insecurities resulting from underdevelopment and political violence inside states.

HUMAN SECURITY: DURING POST COLD WAR ERA

With the end of the Cold War, calls for new thinking in security matters grew rapidly. In 1991, the Stockholm Initiative on

Global Security and Governance issued a call for "Common Responsibility in the 1990's" which referred to "challenges to security other than political rivalry and armaments" and to a "wider concept of security, which deals also with threats that stem from failures in development, environmental degradation, excessive population growth and movement, and lack of progress towards democracy." Four years later, the Commission on Global Governance's report, Our Global Neighborhood, echoed the Stockholm Initiative's words on security: "The concept of global security must be broadened from the traditional focus on the security of states to include the security of people and the security of the planet."

If these commission reports were the precursors to human security thinking, it was only in the early 1990s that an explicitly human security perspective was articulated with some rigor. The first contribution was that of Mahbub ul Haq and the United Nations Development Program (UNDP). Haq, a respected development economist and a long-time consultant to the UNDP, was a central figure in the launching of the human development index (HDI). The human development effort explicitly put at the center of its formulation the notion that development thinking and policies must take as their focus the welfare of individuals rather than simply the macro-economy. The second important intervention on human security was that of the Canadian government and various Canadian academics who led a middle powers' initiative.

To understand these two "schools" or "approaches" and to clarify the difference between human security and traditional national security conceptions, it is necessary to resort to some common terms of reference. The political scientist, David Baldwin, has argued that in order to evaluate the debate over the conception of security, it is vital to define the term more closely. This requires, at the very least, two things: agreement on the root meaning of security; and greater specification of the term, with reference to a series of questions: security for whom, security for which values, how much security, security from what threats, and security by what means?

First of all, the analyst needs a basic understanding of what constitutes the security problem. Here Baldwin takes as a starting point Arnold Wolfers' famous discussion of security as "the absence of threat to acquired values" and modifies this to read "a low probability of damage to acquired values." Security policies are those actions one takes to reduce or limit the probability of damage to one's acquired values. This leaves open a number of vital questions that Baldwin argues must be answered if the term security is to be analytically and prescriptively useful. At least two questions are fundamental: *security for whom* and *security of which values?* These, he notes, "suffice to define the concept of security," but "they provide little guidance for its pursuit". Thus in addition, the analyst should ask: how much security, from what threats, by what means, at what cost, and in what time period?

MAHBUB UL HAQ AND THE UNDP APPROACH TO HUMAN SECURITY

To understand the UNDP approach to human security, let us try to answer the four key questions which have been extracted from the Baldwin schema: Security for whom? Security for which values? Security from what threats? Security by what means?

MAHBUB HAQ AND HUMAN SECURITY

The idea of human security is generally thought to go back to the United Nations Development Program report of 1994. Closely associated with the idea from the beginning was the consulting economist, the late Mahbub ul Haq, who had earlier played a key role in the construction of the Human Development Index (HDI) and who was subsequently the moving force behind the more recent Humane Governance Index (HGI). Haq's approach is outlined in his paper, 'New Imperatives of Human Security'.

Haq answers the question of "security for whom" quite simply. Human security is not about states and nations, but about individuals and people. Thus, he argues that the world is "entering a new era of human security" in which "the entire concept of security will change—and change dramatically". In this new conception, security will be equated with the "security of individuals, not just security of their nations" or, to put it differently, "security of people, not just security of territory." Elsewhere, more normatively, he writes, "We need to fashion a new concept of human security that is reflected in the lives of our people, not in the weapons of our country."

In fashioning this new concept, what values will we seek to protect? Haq is not explicit on this issue, but clearly individual safety and well being in the broad sense are the prime values. Whereas the traditional conception of security emphasizes territorial integrity and national independence as the primary values that need to be protected, human security pertains above all to the safety and well-being of "all the people everywhere — in their homes, in their jobs, in their streets, in their communities, in their environment".

What are the major threats to these values? Here Haq initially essays a brief, illustrative laundry list of threats: drugs, disease, terrorism, and poverty. Later in the essay, in his discussion of what is to be done to advance the cause of human security, it is clear, at least by implication, that a far more fundamental threat exists, namely, an unequal world order in which some states and elites dominate to the detriment of the vast mass of humanity. This world order is embodied in the prevailing conceptions and practices of development, the reliance on arms for security, the divide between North and South globally, and the increasing marginalization of global institutions (e.g. the UN and the Bretton Woods arrangements).

What then is to be done? How can human security be achieved? This is the major part of Haq's contribution, and it is a radical program. Fundamentally, human security will be achieved through "development, not ... through arms." In particular, five rather radical steps are necessary to give life to the new conception of security: a human development conception with emphasis on equity, sustainability, and grassroots participation; a peace dividend to underwrite the broader agenda of human security; a new partnership between North and South based on "justice, not charity" which emphasizes "equitable access to global market opportunities" and economic restructuring; a new framework of global governance built on reform of international institutions such as the IMF, World Bank, and United Nations; and finally, a growing role for global civil society.

Haq outlines a long list of truly far-reaching proposals for global human security. These include:

- *Developmentally:* Sustainability; equity of opportunities (better distribution of productive assets, including land and credit; open access to market opportunities; job creation; social safety nets); and global justice via a "major restructuring" of the world's income, consumption, and lifestyle patterns.

- *Militarily:* Reducing arms expenditures; closing all military bases; converting military aid to economic aid; stopping arms transfers; eliminating arms export subsidies; retraining workers in defense industries.
- *North-South restructuring:* Equitable access to global markets for the poor countries built on the removal of trade barriers (especially in textiles and agriculture); financial compensation from the rich countries in return for immigration controls and for overuse of global environmental resources; and a global payment mechanisms for various services rendered (e.g. environmental services, control of narcotics and disease), for "damages" in cases of economic injury, and for bad economic conduct (e.g. encouraging the brain drain, restricting migration of low-skill labor, export restrictions).
- *Institutionally:* The resuscitation and restructuring of the IMF, World Bank, and UN to focus more on human development; economic adjustments which target the rich more than the poor; new governance patterns everywhere which empower the poor; new institutions such as a world central bank, a global taxation system, a world trade organization, an international investment trust, a world treasury, and above all, a representative and veto-less Economic Security Council in the UN which would be the "highest decision making forum" to deal with "all issues confronting humanity" including food and environmental security, poverty and job creation, migration and drug trafficking.
- *The evolution of a global civil society:* All of the above would require grassroots participation and a change from authoritarian to democratic government.

THE UNDP AND HUMAN SECURITY

The UNDP Report answers the question of "security for whom" by reference to traditional notions of security. Traditional notions of security were concerned with "security of territory from external aggression, or as protection of national interests in foreign policy, or as global security from the threat of nuclear holocaust. It has been related more to nation-states than to people." What this conception overlooked was "the legitimate concerns of ordinary people who sought security in their daily lives." Human security, on the other hand, is "people-centered." Thus, the Report insists, as did Haq that the referent object of human security is individual or people. In support of this contention, the Report cites the founding document of the UN and its original delineation of security as "freedom from fear" as also "freedom from want" and "the equal weight to territories and to people" that that distinction implied. Unfortunately, during the Cold War, security thinking had tilted overly towards the protection of territory; after the Cold War, the Report proposes, it is time to redress the balance and include the protection of people.

The Report's treatment of security values is in two parts. It, first of all, makes a number of rather general statements about values which emphasize the safety, well being, and dignity of individual human beings in their daily lives. Thus, reminiscent of Haq the Report notes that the traditional conception of security, in focussing on territorial integrity, the advancement of the national interest, and nuclear deterrence, ignored clear and more present dangers faced at every turn by ordinary men and women: "For many... security symbolized protection from the threat of disease, hunger, unemployment, crime, social conflict, political repression, and environmental hazards." Less abstractly, "human security is a child who did not die, a disease that did not spread, a job that was not cut, an ethnic tension that did not explode in violence, a dissident who was not silenced. Human security is not a concern with weapons—it is a concern with human life and dignity ... It is concerned with how people live and breathe in a society, how freely they exercise their many choices, how much access they have to market and social opportunities—and whether they live in conflict or in peace." Human security also encompasses a sense of personal choice and surety about the future and of personal efficacy and opportunity. Thus, in drawing attention to the difference between human security and its cognate, human development, the Report argues that the latter is a "broader concept" and refers to "a process of widening the range of people's choices," while the former implies that "people can exercise these choices safely and freely—and that they can be relatively confident that the opportunities they have today are not totally lost tomorrow". Along with a sense of choice and surety about the future, people should be efficacious and empowered enough to be "able to take care of themselves: all people should have the opportunity to meet their most essential needs and to earn their own living."

Economic security refers to an individual's enjoyment of a basic income, either through gainful employment or from a social safety net. Food security refers to an individual's access to food via his or her assets, employment, or income. Health security refers to an individual's freedom from various diseases and debilitating illnesses and his or her access to health care. Environmental security refers to the integrity of land, air, and water, which make human habitation possible. Personal security refers to an individual's freedom from crime and violence, especially women and children who are more vulnerable. Community security refers to cultural dignity and to inter-community peace within which an individual lives and grows. Finally, political security refers to protection against human rights violations.

What are the threats to these human security values? The Report appears to distinguish between two sets of threats. First of all, some threats are more localized. These are threats that are particular to different societies or regions of the world and seemingly vary by level of economic development and geographical location. Secondly, some threats are global in nature because "threats within countries rapidly spill beyond national frontiers.

According to the Report, the more localized threats can be understood in relation to the seven values of human security. These are summarized below:

- *Threats to economic security*: Lack of productive and remunerative employment, precarious employment, absence of publicly financed safety nets.
- *Threats to food security*: Lack of food entitlements including insufficient access to assets, work, and assured incomes
- *Threats to health security*: Infectious and parasitic diseases, diseases of the circulatory system and cancers, lack of safe water, air pollution, lack of access to health care facilities.
- *Threats to environmental security*: Declining water availability, water pollution, declining arable land,

deforestation, desertification, air pollution, natural disasters.

- *Threats to personal security*: Violent crime, drug trafficking, violence and abuse of children and women.
- *Threats to community security:* Breakdown of the family, collapse of traditional languages and cultures, ethnic discrimination and strife, genocide and ethnic cleansing.
- *Threats to political security*: Government repression, systematic human rights violations, militarization.

In addition to the more localized threats listed above, the Report cites a number of more global or transnational threats whose spread or effects go well beyond any given national boundaries. These are grouped into six areas:

- Population growth which increases the pressure on non-renewable resources and is linked intimately to global poverty, environmental degradation, and international migration.
- Growing disparities in global income leading to overconsumption and overproduction in the industrialized countries and poverty and environmental degradation in the developing world.
- Increasing international migration as a function of population growth, poverty, and the policies of the industrial countries have contributed to the flow of international migrants as also an increase in refugees and internally displaced persons.
- Various forms of environmental decay (that among other things cause acid rain, skin cancer, and global warming) as well as reduced biodiversity, and the destruction of wetlands, coral reefs, and temperate forests as well as tropical rainforests.
- Drug trafficking, which has grown into a global, multinational industry.
- International terrorism which has spread from Latin America in the 1960s to a global phenomenon.

Given this enormous array of values to be protected and threats to be combated, what exactly needs to be done? How should the world community respond? Traditional security threats could be dealt with by nuclear and conventional weapons, alliances and balances of power, as well as great power and UN intervention. The new security agenda demands a much wider range of instrumentalities and cooperation between a greater range of actors—and certainly there is little place for the use of force. Among others, the Report recommends endorsement of the concept of human security itself, changes in national and international policy focused on basic needs, productive and remunerative employment and human rights, preventive diplomacy and "preventive" development, and the reform of global institutions.

References

Booth, K. (ed.), Critical Security Studies and World Politics (Boulder, Co: Lynne Rienner), 2005.

Human Security Centre, Human Security Report Project (Vancouver: The University of British Columbia), 2008.

Jolly, Richard and Deepayan Basu, The Human Security Framework and National Human Development Reports, UNDP, May 2006.

King, Gary and Christopher Murray, "Rethinking Human Security", *Political Science Quarterly*, Volume 116, Number 4, 2001-02.

Krause, K., "Towards a Practical Human Security Agenda", Policy Paper 26 (Geneva: Geneva Centre for the Democratic Control of Armed Forces), 2007.

Mahbub ul Haq, "New Imperatives of Human Security," RGICS Paper No. 17, Rajiv Gandhi Institute for Contemporary Studies (RGICS) (New Delhi: Rajiv Gandhi Foundation), 1994.

Neville Yeomans, On Global Reform and International Normative Model Areas *(Inma)* February 2007. http://www.laceb.org.au/gri.htm

Thakur, R.,"Human Security Regimes" in Tow, W. Thakur, R. and Hyun, I. T. (eds.), Asia's Emerging Regional Order: Reconciling Traditional and Human Security (New York: United Nations Press), 2000.

Thomas, C., Gold Governance, Development and Human Security: The Challenge of Poverty and Inequality (London: Pluto Press), 2000.

United Nations Development Program (UNDP), "Redefining Security: The Human Dimension", *Current History*, Vol. 94, 1994.

United Nations Development Programme's (UNDP) Human Development Report 1994.

Index